PRACTICAL CROSS COUNTRY

A Rider's Guide to Hunter Trials

PRACTICAL CROSS COUNTRY

A Rider's Guide to Hunter Trials

Jane Holderness-Roddam

Photography by Bob Langrish

WARD LOCK

A Ward Lock Book

First published in the UK 1994
by Ward Lock
A Cassell Imprint
Villiers House
41/47 Strand
London
WC2N 5JE

Copyright © Ward Lock 1994

Distributed in the United States
by Sterling Publishing Co., Inc.
387 Park Avenue South, New York, NY 10016-8810

Distributed in Australia
by Capricorn Link (Australia) Pty Ltd
P.O. Box 665, Lane Cove, NSW 2066

A British Library Cataloguing in Publication Data block for this book
may be obtained from the British Library

ISBN 0-7063-7134-8

Printed and bound in Great Britain by Hillmans (Frome) Ltd.

CONTENTS

Acknowledgements

I would like to thank Bob Langrish for his patience and care with the photography for this book, and Sandra McCallum for typing the manuscript.

Also Darrell Scaife, Sue Green, Franziska Lewinski, Lisa Harrowsmith, Vicky Penman, Nadine Ronan, Judy Long and Vicky Gordon-Ingram for their help with the pictures.

I am also indebted to Nick Bush for allowing us to take some of the cross country photographs over his UK Chasers Course at Shirehill and Mr and Mrs Sanderson for those taken at their Fern Farm Cross Country Course near Swindon.

Jane Holderness-Roddam

INTRODUCTION

Riding is more popular today than ever before, both as a leisure pastime and as a competitive sport. There is something for everyone, whether you want a relaxing hobby or the thrill of competing.

There are numerous different sports for the rider to take up once the basic skills of control, balance and co-ordination have been mastered. For me, as a child, learning to ride was relatively easy as it nearly always is when one is young with no pre-conceived ideas. But starting young is not essential - one can learn to ride at any age.

I have few recollections of that early period of my riding career but do remember falling off my pony endlessly because I would not loosen the reins when he wanted to eat, so over his ears I would go! Later I went hunting and the thrill of galloping across country and jumping fences at speed really captured my imagination.

To this day I have a little musical box won at a hunter trial for being the best competitor under ten years round the senior hunter trials. I was eight at the time and I have no idea whether there was anyone else as young or even if I actually completed the course. From then on hunter trials and cross country riding were for me, and this no doubt set the scene which eventually led to an Olympic gold medal 12 years later.

For those who want the competitive life there can be few better ways to start than sponsored or fun rides and then competition in the relaxed and informal atmosphere of hunter trials. It may not lead to a gold medal but something equally important will be achieved in terms of fun and sense of purpose, and for many it will be the start of a whole new world of equestrian achievements and a unique partnership between horse and rider.

CHAPTER 1

THE BASICS

How it all began

Hunter trials have been part of the equestrian scene for years but there seems to be some confusion as to when they actually began. Certainly, they were being held long before World War 1. Several famous octogenarians, who attended the famous army training school at Weedon, recall going off to

Hunter trials are enjoyable and give people of all ages and experience the chance to feel what it is like to compete over cross country jumps. This horse and rider look full of confidence over this bullfinch fence and are already looking towards the next one.

hunter trials with the same objectives that we have today, of teaching the horse to go across country and of having fun.

In those days hunting was the principal equestrian sport and every good hunter had to be safe across country, so, presumably, hunts initially organized the competitions to give horses the chance to learn to be good performers. Point to points were much more varied in those days, with the riders being given written instructions to meet at a particular point, usually a church, from where further instructions were issued to ride across country to the next point, hence the name point to point. The varied ground and fences in between were often quite daunting but you soon knew what sort of horse you had if he coped well!

Britain is unique in the huge number of hunter trials, sponsored rides, team chases, hunting, drag hunting, etc. that it has to offer the rider. Particularly in the winter, not a weekend goes by without numerous competitions, which are organized, either by hunts or other bodies, throughout the season, which generally runs from September through to April. The summer is reserved for horse shows, events and show jumping.

In certain states of the USA, hunter pace competitions take place, which are judged more on the style and way of going of the horse and rider, with riding to an optimum time being a main objective. As in Britain, fox hunting and drag hunting are also very popular here, but, as yet, the fun ride or sponsored ride has not caught on. New Zealand and Australia also run numerous similar competitions.

Hunter trials

Hunter trials are mostly organized into classes to cater for different standards of horse and rider and usually have a small course to start with, varying in height from 76 to 91 cm (2 ft 6 in – 3 ft), with either a pairs class or a junior one to follow over the same size of course. The last class is usually over a bigger course, for more experienced horses and riders. The fences vary in height, according to class rules, from around 99 cm up to 106 cm (3 ft 3 in – 3 ft 6 in). At some events the course can be up to 114 cm (3 ft 9 in) in the open section. Some hunter trials finish the day with a team chase.

Many hunter trials divide the courses into a junior day followed by one for seniors. Classes are divided by age and the height of the fences. Sometimes they are judged on a clear round nearest the 'bogey' time, which is usually based on

what is described as 'a fair hunting pace' or strong canter/slow gallop. Other competitions have a timed section in the course, which sometimes includes opening and shutting a gate, with the winner being the rider with the fastest time through this section, who has also gone clear.

Occasionally, hunter trials and team chases amalgamate, with the former running a single and/or pairs class over the course before the team of (usually) four horses with only the first three to finish counting in the final result. The third horse's time thus determines the winning team.

Pairs classes are enormous fun and a great way to get started in the sport, especially if you go with a more experienced

Pairs classes are a wonderful way to get started. By going with a more experienced horse or rider you can get the feel of hunter trials.

competitor who can jolly you along and give encouragement and advice on the way round! Usually, there are certain 'dressing fences', at which you get either bonus or penalty marks for the horses being together (or not) over the fence. The specific rules as to how these are judged are normally clearly written in the schedule. The course may also include a timed section or require a clear round nearest to the bogey time or, occasionally, just the fastest time wins.

Although hunter trials have been in existence for so long, there are as yet no specific rules. The British Horse Society is currently considering making its own guidelines for horse trials available to the organizers of amateur competitions, which may help towards improving the standards of safety and giving uniformity in course building and the provision of emergency cover. In general, these competitions are well organized but it is up to the competitor to look through the schedule before entering, to ensure that the provision of at least basic medical and veterinary services will be on site, not just on call, throughout the day and also to check, on the day, that the course is well built. The standard of fences varies tremendously but they should look solid and be safe, which is generally the case at the majority of events. An experienced course builder will ensure that a good standard is produced for all courses. The horse respects a fence more and can judge it better if it is strong and solid-looking, while he may not be so careful over a poorly constructed or 'spindly' course. It should also be possible to dismantle a fence quickly in the rare event of a horse becoming trapped if things go wrong.

General rules

All hunter trials follow a set of rules that are applicable to that particular competition, rather than a standardized rule book covering all events, so what might be applicable to one is not necessarily the case at the next. It really is vital that you read the rules for each outing carefully, to ensure what you have to remember for that particular day. Although the following list of rules and conditions looks rather long, I have included most of the normal ones likely to be found in the majority of schedules.

Typical rules and conditions of entry for hunter trials and team chases in the UK

1   Three refusals at any one fence will eliminate the horse and rider.

2 If, at any time, before or during the competition, a horse appears to be sick or exhausted, it may be eliminated on the authority of the on-duty veterinary officer or an official of the course.

3 Competitors must jump fences in numerical order, keeping all red flags on their right and white flags on their left. Any horse taking the wrong course will be eliminated.

4 After two falls, a competitor must retire. If they continue they will be eliminated.

5 Any horse that has been eliminated or is retiring must leave the course at a walk.

6 A time limit will be set for completion of the course. (Team classes – any team whose first three members exceed this time will be eliminated and must retire from the course. Any team member overtaken by a member of a following team must retire.)

7 No horse is allowed to compete more than once in any class, except in minimus classes.

8 In the event of a tie, the prize money will be divided.

9 Hunting dress or a team uniform must be worn. All competitors must wear skull caps of a recognized safety standard and a stock. Back protectors are recommended.

10 Competitors may exercise their horses only in the area provided.

11 Riders and owners of horses must obey any order or direction given by an authorized official of the event.

12 Please telephone the secretary to obtain your starting times etc. on .... between the hours of .... No times will be given outside of these hours. Failure to declare your team/horse will result in your place being given to someone on the waiting list. Car passes will be sent only on receipt of a stamped, addressed envelope. In the event of an entered rider/team withdrawing from the competition before the starting time, no refund of entry fees will be made.

13 The order of running will be drawn and any team or rider failing to start at their appointed time, for any reason, will be eliminated and their entry fees forfeited. A team or rider so eliminated will, however, be allowed to ride the course on an 'hors concours' basis at the end of the competition, should time so permit.

14 The organizers reserve the right to:
(a) Cancel or postpone the event for any reason if they see fit. In the event of a postponement, no entry fees will be refunded.

(b) Withhold any prize if there are insufficient entries.

(c) Refuse any entry without stating a reason.

(d) Alter the advertised times of the event.

(e) Alter the course or omit any obstacle at any time before or during the competition.

(f) Eliminate any rider or riders not adhering to these rules or failing to follow the directions of the officials.

15 In the event of cancellation, the following refunds of entry fees will be made. Class .., full refund/cheques destroyed. Classes .., a refund, less an administration charge of £.. per team will be made.

16 The organizers and landowners will not accept any liability for accidents, damage, injury to horses, riders, owners or spectators or any property whatsoever. All vehicles are parked at owner's risk.

17 Small children must be kept off the course and under control of a responsible adult at all times.

18 Dogs must be kept on leads at all times.

Scoring

In the majority of events, the following horse trials scoring system is now adopted, although some events will make up their own adaptations. This table is the one generally in use, for faults such as refusals, run outs, circling in front of, or round, a fence and falls:

1st refusal, run out or circle of horse at obstacle – 20 penalties

2nd refusal, run out or circle of horse at obstacle – 40 penalties

3rd refusal, run out or circle of horse at same obstacle – Elimination

Fall of horse and/or rider at obstacle – 60 penalties

2nd fall of horse and/or rider on the course – Elimination

Error of course not rectified – Elimination

Omission of obstacle or boundary flag – Elimination

Retaking an obstacle already jumped – Elimination

Jumping obstacle in wrong order – Elimination

The fence judges are briefed on what is classed as a refusal, run out or circle in doubtful situations, particularly in the case of a horse stopping in front of a fence, having a good look, then jumping. If he steps back, even with one foot, this is classed as a refusal. Remember that you are on top and so won't be able to see or probably feel what all four legs are doing, so do not argue with the poor judges – they know what they see and they write it down straightaway – there is always another day!

'A fall is an awful thing!'. The rider is probably going to hit the ground and will incur 60 penalties.

The illustrations overleaf should help to clarify problems that can sometimes occur if you miss a fence because the horse runs out to the side or, in the case of combination fences (two or more elements), if you circle or cross your tracks in between, which can happen through lack or control or insufficient steering!

Combination fences sited close together will be considered as one obstacle and will have an A and B on the two parts or, occasionally, even a third part (C). At these parts you cannot have more than two refusals or run outs before incurring elimination.

15

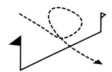

0 penalties
Not presented initially

20 penalties
Presented and circled

20 penalties
Presented and circled

Adjacent fences numbered 16 and 17

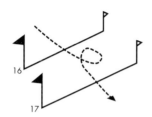
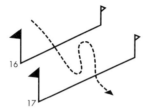
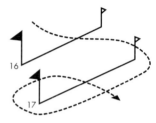

0 penalties
Not presented at 17

20 penalties
Presented at 17

0 penalties
Not presented at 17 initially

Combination fence 16 ab

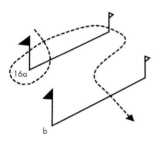
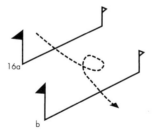
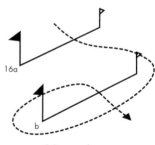

20 penalties
Circled

20 penalties
Circled

20 penalties
Circled

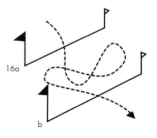

20 penalties

It is important to know how
penalties are judged so that you
do not cross your tracks or circle
in front of or between certain
fences that are close together.

When can you compete?

If you have never competed in a hunter trial before it is important that you ride at a suitable standard and that your horse is sufficiently prepared and schooled to be able to jump the course easily.

One of the best ways to start is to go on a fun ride or sponsored ride, usually organized in aid of a local charity, which includes optional cross country fences. These are usually advertised in the local papers, tack shops and riding schools. If you go along with a friend or two and can jump the majority of fences you encounter that are of the same size as those you are likely to meet at the hunter trial, then you can feel fairly confident that you are ready.

Remember that your horse must do the course alone unless you are starting in a pairs class, so you must feel confident when out on your own. Being herd animals, horses will often be happy to go round with another horse but may not be quite so keen going solo. You may well find that you are not so brave on your own either, so do not rush the competing bit until you are confident that you can cope! Confidence is the key ingredient and it comes through practice and never doing more than you are safely capable of at any particular time. A gradual build-up, with plenty of practice and help on hand to explain what to do and where to go, is vital at the beginning of your competitive career.

The ability and standard of your horse will determine much of what you can and cannot do. An efficient and confident jockey on a young, inexperienced horse will help that horse to gain confidence and move on but this could prove disastrous with an inexperienced rider, whereas an inexperienced rider on a really experienced horse will be able to do things much more easily and quicker if they feel confident and under control on such an animal.

Those who have hunted or drag hunted a good deal will have learnt so much about control and balance and how to cope in different types of going that they will have a great advantage over others who have not done this, as their knowledge has been gained naturally, through experience. No amount of reading or drilling in an arena can make up for having to react quickly to the unknown situations that are encountered all the time out hunting.

In the UK, we are very lucky in having numerous excellent cross country training courses. Recently, UK Chasers courses have sprung up throughout Britain, adding to those already in existence, and now it is possible to practise regularly over well-constructed, small fences of different designs almost every weekend throughout the year. The USA also has many excellent training areas, where riders can hire fences to school over.

The right horse

The horse or pony you want to compete on must be fit, sound, healthy, of calm disposition and trained sufficiently well to be capable of putting in a reasonable performance. Obviously, it is irresponsible to take along an animal that is out of control, which then becomes a danger not only to you but, more important, to spectators and other riders as well. This also goes for an animal plainly not ready, nor sufficiently trained, to do the sport. Whether a beginner or reasonably experienced, make sure you have been to watch a few events so that you are fully conversant with what is involved and how things are run before venturing off yourself. Always take someone with you or, at least, let the secretary know you are on your own in case anything untoward happens to you or your horse.

All sorts of horses and ponies compete very successfully in hunter trials, varying from native ponies, such as Welsh, New Forest, Connemara, to Arabs and even the occasional heavy breeds – plus, of course, combinations of any of these. There are no hard and fast rules, except that the horse must be right for you – the rider. This includes his size, strength and ability. There is nothing worse than seeing a rider overhorsed (small or inexperienced jockey on a huge and very strong horse) and such combinations invariably lead to disaster at some stage. Likewise, the combination of large jockeys on small or weak horses very rarely works successfully as, more often than not, the horse ends up stopping as he is unable to jump successfully with the weight of the rider moving about in the saddle, unless they remain in perfect balance throughout.

The horse should be easily managed by the rider. He should be a safe and confident jumper, controllable even when going downhill and have been prepared for competition so that he is fit and capable. He also needs well-fitting tack that is suitable for the occasion, and must be sound, with recently and well-shod feet.

One of the most important factors is the horse's temperament. He must be willing and kind and must not become

The horse should be the right size for the rider and should be easily manageable even when going down steep hills.

overexcited. Any sport where speed is involved requires a horse with an equitable nature. You do not want to have to cope with a highly strung, overexcitable animal every time you go out. Obviously, any fit horse is going to be a little on his toes once he knows what he is in for but most will usually remain quite calm as long as you keep walking round quietly on a loose rein. Some riders hang on tightly to their horses' heads for ages before setting off, which is not only thoughtless but also uncomfortable for the horse and why you see some poor animals rearing and plunging around, especially at the start when everyone gets a little nervous. Leave

19

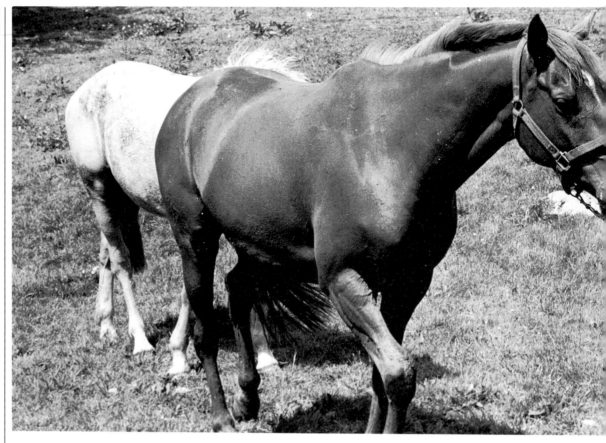

The horse's temperament is very important, so watch him in as many different situations as possible. If you are to keep the horse out at grass ensure that he is easy to catch.

your horse's head alone as much as possible and, when you do pull, do so with soft, elastic fingers rather than a ham-fisted hard pull with your whole hand.

Buying a horse

Always make finding out about the horse's temperament your first priority. Examine the horse thoroughly and do not take for granted anything you are told by the vendor. Always see him ridden first before trying him yourself, to ensure that he looks safe and sensible. See him run up in hand and stand behind to see if he moves reasonably straight; then see him come towards you at walk and trot. A horse that swings legs in every direction rarely stands up to hard, competitive work for long – you would need your vet's advice about this if you really liked everything else about him.

Make sure you know what the horse is like in traffic if this is relevant to where you live. It is a good idea to go out for a hack with another horse, if the vendors can do that, or see him

ridden out and follow in the car. Try to see the horse doing all the sorts of things you want to do with him yourself. Do not be fobbed off with the story – 'Sorry we have no jumps' – this usually means he does not jump! Other classics are seeing horses in a muddy field so that you never see their feet properly – this may indicate odd or boxy feet, which is not good! 'No rider' may mean he is unrideable – do not be the next one on the floor!

If the horse is tacked up and ready on your arrival, 'so as to be ready when you come', this can indicate that he is difficult to tack up because he bites or other horrors. A horse that is tied up on your arrival may weave or crib bite.

Seeing him lunged before the owner gets on 'because it's only young' usually indicates a difficult horse or one that is cold-backed. If he is really ready to be sold on, the horse should have got past that stage. Do not be afraid to ask about the horse. If there is a helper around, ask them as well – often little things come out that can set warning bells ringing.

Having said all this, one must remember that the majority of people are honest and truthful and might say or do any of the above in total innocence. However, when you have been in the game of buying and selling horses for as long as I have, you get wise to all the pitfalls and, unfortunately, there are plenty of unscrupulous dealers and other individuals around who make their money out of the unwary and relatively inexperienced.

It is always a good idea to take a knowledgeable friend along with you if possible, who knows what is suitable for you and may even ride the animal as well. Very often first impressions stick – if you liked what you saw initially and he did everything you wanted – fine.

However, if this is your first horse, you might be so excited that you would think that about anything, so be sensible and always arrange for a veterinary examination, which will give you the satisfaction of knowing that the horse is normal in eye, heart, wind and limb and, in the vet's opinion, suitable for the purpose for which you are buying. This certificate can also be used for insurance purposes in most cases, as long as this is done straightaway.

Buying a horse is expensive and it is worth considering insurance as accidents and thefts do happen (the latter are on the increase) and vets' fees can also be very expensive. There are various types of cover to cater for most needs and many that give cover for death, theft, fire, etc., and also vets' fees. These are particularly popular with one-horse owners. Most equine insurance companies advertise in equestrian magazines but do make sure you are dealing with a well-established company with a good name, not one that has only been in business a short time. Check what is involved before rushing off to collect your new horse – he should be covered before you collect him in case the unexpected happens on the journey home.

Where to keep your horse

There are three main ways of being able to compete and ride. You may share with a friend, ride a horse from a local riding school at which you have been riding regularly, although not all allow this or are insured to do it, or you can ride your own horse, which is, or course, much the most satisfying way!

In the latter situation, you may keep your horse at home, either stabled, part-stabled or out at grass, or away at livery.

Many horses and ponies are ridden from the field. They should be fine as long as they are getting enough food for the work they are doing. A New Zealand rug can be put on in the cold weather, and a trace or blanket clip would be ideal if they get hot when worked.

If you share with a friend, this probably means that the horse is kept with them or is stabled locally, possibly at livery. With a riding school horse, the problem of how or where to keep him does not exist but then you do not share quite the same enjoyment (or worry!) of tending and caring for him either. Obviously, this is a time-consuming job as animals require constant supervision, which could be quite impractical for many people.

There are many different ways of looking after your horse, depending on your lifestyle and time you have available. Generally, horses are creatures of habit and will adapt very happily to whatever routine is adopted but do try to stick to one method if possible.

Much time and effort goes into keeping a horse and this can be made as easy or as difficult as you wish but, as long as the basic essentials mentioned below are carried out conscientiously, the horse should be quite happy and should serve you as a loyal friend for many years to come.

General stable management

General day-to-day care and management of a horse require a certain knowledge and understanding of his basic daily needs. The most important of these is a regular supply of food, water and exercise. It is also necessary to understand a little of how the horse thinks and how he expresses his likes and dislikes. In the wild, horses are herd animals, so they are much happier in groups than on their own. A nervous horse will often follow another willingly but be really silly if by himself.

The horse must learn to trust his owner and will generally do this quite quickly if a regular routine is adopted. He learns best through repetition and will quickly come to realize that a certain time of day is feed time or the time he gets turned out or whatever.

Depending on what your plans are for your horse, it is important that he is fit enough for the demands to be placed on him. If you want to jump your horse, he must have received the right build-up of work beforehand, so that he will be fit enough to carry out your wishes easily. If he is not being ridden daily, he will still require exercise, either in the form of being turned out or lunged. You may, of course, keep him out in the field anyway or housed in a large barn, which will give him the freedom to move around and to exercise by himself.

Feeding and watering

Feeding horses is a complex subject as every animal must be treated as an individual but, as long as your horse is looking well and not too fat, coping with the work he is doing and is being wormed regularly, then you are probably not too far out with your feeding programme.

Remember that the golden rules of feeding include the following:

1 Feed little and often. The horse has a relatively small stomach, so it is best to give him two or three smaller feeds rather than one large one. Most people feed their horses morning and evening, with poor feeders having a late feed and/or a lunchtime one as well if necessary. Hay should be freely available.

   Horses out in the field may not need much extra food if there is plenty of grass but will require extra hard feed and/or hay during the autumn and winter, when the goodness (protein) has gone and grass is no longer plentiful. 'Keep' blocks (vitamins and minerals) can be placed in the fields during this time to ensure that the horse obtains all essential vitamins and minerals. Coupled with hay, this is often sufficient for animals that are in light work or resting. A horse that is being worked harder and ridden daily, may require one or two feeds per day, depending on his type.

2 Always ensure that plenty of fresh water is available at all times, except immediately prior to riding or competing. When travelling or in hot weather, horses will require extra fluid to compensate for the effects of dehydration, so always take water with you when travelling. If your horse lives out all year round, keep a good check on his water trough to ensure that it is filling properly and, in freezing weather, make sure the ice is broken up daily. Careful lagging of the inlet pipe will help to keep this unfrozen. Fresh streams must be clean and have easy, safe access for the horse if a trough is not available. Owners who have to refill water containers daily must ensure that this is done conscientiously by others if they are ever away. Never allow your horse to drink while he is still hot or puffing after exercise. He should always be walked until cool and then allowed small, but frequent, drinks until he is satisfied, one-quarter to half a bucket at a time. Long drinks of cold water could cause colic in a hot horse.

3 Feed your horse according to the work being done. If he is

Remember to treat your horse as an individual and feed him according to the work he is doing.

not in work, or is missing a normal day's exercise, reduce the concentrates to prevent a build-up of protein etc. in his system. Give a bran mash once or twice a week and whenever he is unable to get exercise. It is always safer to give too little rather than too much, especially to the stabled horse that is confined to his box. Good quality hay should always be freely available, however, except immediately prior to exercise or competing.

4 Keep to a routine and feed top quality feed and hay only. Musty hay can cause serious damage to the lungs of the horse, which will ultimately affect his breathing and general condition and health. Hay should be fresh-smelling and relatively dust-free. It is normally fed approximately six to eighteen months after it has been made, when it still maintains good feed value. New hay can be rather indigestible. If used before it is four to six months old, it should be introduced gradually into the diet by mixing it with older hay.

5 Always make changes gradually, whether altering the concentrate or the hay rations in the diet. This also goes for new grass. If you are letting your horse out on to fresh pasture in the spring, start by letting him have only a couple of hours if the grass is very lush. In the spring, in particular, grass is at its richest and both ponies and horses could easily get laminitis (inflammation of the lining of the feet associated with too much rich grass and a sudden change of diet), although this can still occur at any other time of year.

6 Never feed your horse immediately prior to exercise and always ensure he is cool after work before giving him a feed. You will know yourself that working on a full stomach does not make it comfortable to do strenuous exercise. The horse's stomach is small and needs time to empty before he is able to work. It can take anything up to six hours to empty completely and at least an hour should be allowed after feeding before normal exercise. At least four hours should be allowed if the horse has to gallop and jump, as in competing, hunting or jumping seriously.

Types of feed

Today, many feeds are manufactured as complete 'mixes', which include all the main requirements necessary for health, including minerals and vitamins. These feeds have been formulated to provide a suitable diet for horses in different types of work and it is important that you choose the right one for the type of horse you have and the sort of work he is doing.

All too often people tend to think upwards with food rather than downwards. If good quality hay is freely available, do be cautious about feeding too high a percentage of protein to your horse. The following is a general guide to your horse's concentrate requirements but too much will do more harm than too little.

9 – 11 per cent protein is usually sufficient for all ponies and most horses in general light work or those ridden at weekends only. Usually fed once or twice a day.

12 – 14 per cent protein is likely to be ample for those who require a little more 'go' and are in general work or hunting or hunter trialling at weekends. If the horse is having two feeds a day and looks well, this is obviously all right. If he looks a little light in condition, add an extra feed or give a little more in each.

15 per cent upwards is designed for horses in more serious work, such as racing or three-day eventing, and is outside the scope of this book in most cases.

16.00 – 16.02 hh hunter/eventer. In at night, out by day

am   900 g (2 lb) cubes or mix (protein content 9–11 per cent)
pm   1.4 kg (3 lb) cubes or mix
late   900 g (2 lb) cubes or mix
(if necessary)
Hay as necessary, according to condition

PC pony, 16.02 hh horse. Stabled

am   675 - 900 g (1½–2 lb) cubes or mix (low protein, 9 per cent)
midday 450 g - 1.4 kg (1–3 lb) cubes or mix
pm   675 g - 1.4 kg (1½–3 lb) cubes or mix
Hay as necessary according to condition

Pony up to 14.2 hh. Out but working hard at weekends and holidays

am   450 g (1 lb) cubes or mix
pm   675 g (1½ lb) cubes or mix   } when in work
Given only if necessary or if the pony is losing condition during the summer on good keep

Sample feeding charts

For those feeding straight foods, the concentrates are as follows:

Oats: the traditional protein food for horses. These are usually fed rolled or bruised but can be a little 'heating', tending to 'hot up' some horses. They are rarely fed to ponies. If you have a rather sluggish horse, who requires more energy, oats are the food to choose.

Barley: now extremely popular, having a similar nutritional value to oats but considered less heating and more suitable for the horse who already has plenty of go. It is a fattening food and high in energy.

Nuts or cubes: available in several types and, like the mixes, produced according to the required protein content. They generally provide a completely balanced diet for the horse. They can be fed as they are, with hay, or as part of the horse's everyday diet, along with other feeds.

Bulk (bran and chaff): these form the main bulk feeds and are usually fed together. A well-dampened bran mash, with added Epsom salts, is normally given once a week to the stabled horse as a laxative or whenever he has not been able to have proper exercise.

Sugarbeet: another bulk food, good for keeping on weight and high in energy. It comes in pellet or pulp-flake form. The pellets will swell to five times their dry size in water and must be soaked for 24 hours. It is likewise essential that the pulp is soaked for at least 12 hours. Half a scoop will absorb at least half to two-thirds of a bucket of water as it also expands dramatically when wet. Never allow a horse to eat sugarbeet dry as it could have fatal results.

Minerals and vitamins: the complete mixes and nuts normally include all the necessary vitamins and minerals already, so it is wasteful, and sometimes harmful, to add a separate supplement to your horse's diet. Occasionally, however, if you feed straight foods that you mix yourself, the horse may require extra, especially if he is stabled and unable to find any natural herbs and minerals to compensate. You can either use a mineral supplement recommended by your vet or buy a mineral block to keep in his manger or in a holder on the wall, which he can lick as he pleases.

In hot weather, or whenever the horse has sweated a lot a little extra salt should be added to the feed. This will help to replace salts lost through evaporation and sweat. Feed one level tablespoon a day, well mixed with the feed.

Succulents: feed these in the form of carrots and apples (cut lengthways so that they will not become stuck in the gullet or throat). These are great favourites with horses and should be added to the feed whenever possible. Apple and carrot peelings from the kitchen are just as popular.

Titbits: beware of feeding 'titbits' regularly to your horse. While the odd 'goodie' is a great treat, horrific accidents have been caused by people feeding these as a habit. The horse may come to expect them and can sometimes become vicious towards you and/or others if you do not produce them, resulting in a nasty bite or kick. Do not turn your horse into a monster. Never allow other people, especially children, to feed your horse anything.

Worming: no amount of careful feeding will work if the horse is full of worms. Worming should be done on a regular basis throughout the year, on a four- to six-weekly routine. Ask your vet for advice on what brands to use and at what time, as it is advisable to vary the types to ensure that every variety of worm is being kept under control. Do not be fooled by the belief that stabled horses do not get worms. While there is less opportunity for them to pick up the larvae from the grass, they

Regular worming is vital to your horse's health. Your vet will advise you on the different brands suitable for your horse.

still are vulnerable to infestation from flies and those worms that are already in their system. Early in their lives some animals suffer damage from worm infestation from which they will never fully recover and many have died early from worm damage caused by lack of regular worming.

Signs of worms include a dull, staring coat and a failure to thrive despite eating well. A pot belly is a sign of bad worm infestation and if this is the case your vet will need to prescribe an intensive worming programme. A dung sample should be sent for a worm count if you are in any doubt about your horse's condition.

Flu vaccinations and tetanus protection

Equine flu, of which there are several different strains, is a frightening disease after which those afflicted are rarely ever as fit again. Flu vaccinations have been highly successful in keeping things under control, even when new strains emerge, as those horses that are protected rarely get the full strength of anything going around.

All horses and ponies should be vaccinated and their records, signed and stamped by your vet, should be kept safe. Following the initial three injections, which have to be given to build up immunity, according to standard veterinary requirements, booster vaccinations should be given annually thereafter. Be very careful to keep these up to date and given at the right time.

At all international competitions, horse trials, dressage competitions, many shows, pony club camps, etc., flu vaccinations are mandatory before horses are allowed on to the site, as is the case for all race meetings and point to points. It is essential for everyone to follow suit to help to keep the equine world free of this virus. Try to give your horse his flu vac when he is having an easy time; as he should not be allowed to get hot or to gallop, preferably for a week, after receiving it.

Tetanus, or lockjaw as it is sometimes known, is a horrific condition caused by a virus that is usually picked up through cuts and puncture wounds. It can be protected against by vaccine and this is usually given in conjunction with the flu vaccine, with a bi-annual booster. Every horse and pony should be protected, as should every human who works on a farm or at a stable and faces the likelihood of cutting themselves on the old machinery, rusty wire, etc., so often found around such places.

Shoeing

Every working horse must have his feet regularly attended to and those in the fields that are not working will need periodic trims, at approximately six- to eight-week intervals, to ensure their feet stay in shape and do not start to break up, leading to lameness.

Generally, a working horse needs shoeing every four to six weeks. Some will require attention more often but few should go for longer than six weeks without the shoes being removed, the horn trimmed and the shoe replaced or, if worn, new ones put on. How much and how often this is done very much depends on the horse's movement and the sort of work being done. If he is out on roadwork a lot, the horse is likely to require attention more frequently than when he is no longer doing that type of work.

The hoof must be square on the ground and the angle of the pastern and the front of the hoof should be the same.

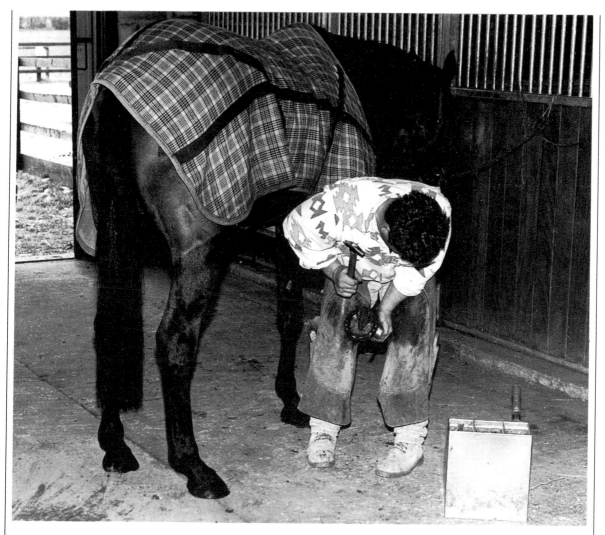

It is essential that the horse's foot stays in balance and, if the horse is to stay sound it must be regularly checked to see that the angle of the foot is correct and that the shape is uniform. Many animals go lame because they are not shod regularly enough.

For horses competing on slippery ground, you can ask your farrier to provide stud holes into which you can screw studs of different sizes to give him extra grip. Many horses feel much more secure and will jump better in slippery conditions with these 'grips'.

Studs are put in on arrival at the event and taken out again immediately afterwards. It is wrong to leave them in when the horse is in the trailer or horsebox for long, or when travelling, as he could injure himself by treading on the opposite

Keep your horse's feet in good condition and shape with regular shoeing and trimming.

31

Right: Studs can be used for extra grip and are inserted as shown. Remember to inform your farrier that you require stud holes so that he puts them in the shoe. Plug the holes with oiled cotton wool ready for use.

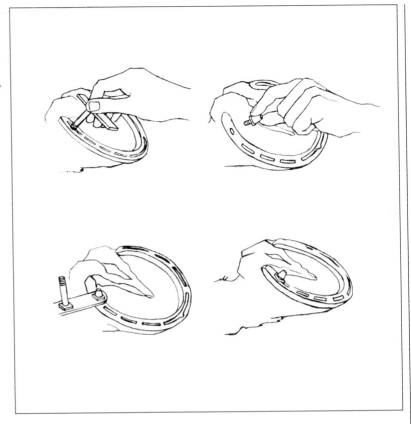

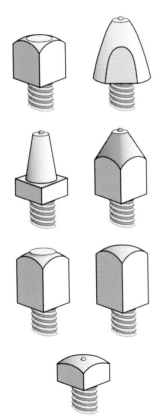

foot or when cornering. Generally, in Britain, studs are placed towards the outside, near the heel of the shoe, but in America and other countries they are often put on the inside of the shoe as well. As a general rule small studs are used for hard ground and large ones in deeper going.

A nail to clean out the holes, a 'tap' to ensure the thread is clear and a spanner to tighten the studs in place are necessary, along with a selection of studs and some oiled cotton wool to plug the holes as soon as you take out the studs. This allows you to clean them out easily before you use them next time. It is sensible to plug the holes with freshly oiled wool the day before the event to save time, as the studs will then go in quicker and much more easily.

Clipping

For most horses in competitive work, it will be necessary to clip or part-clip them once they have their winter coat if they are not to sweat excessively and lose condition. Careful thought needs to be given to this, depending on whether the horse is stabled and going to remain in for the winter, where it is possible to keep him warm, or whether he is to go out at the end of the season or for the winter, when he will need all his coat to keep warm, even if wearing a New Zealand rug.

Several types of clip can be used to solve these problems, ranging from a hunter clip to merely taking off the hair up the neck and under the body. If your horse is getting very hot but you are only going to be riding him for another few weeks, it is pointless to take all his coat off, so you can choose a clip that just keeps him comfortable and perhaps you could regulate your work to give him a few more breaks so that he will not become particularly hot.

A **trace clip** is ideal for horses that live out most or all of the year as this keeps the top of the horse warm, which is the most important and vulnerable part in cold weather, yet leaves the part most likely to sweat free of a thick coat. A New Zealand rug can be put on as soon as the weather turns cold.

Some horses sweat a lot and may need a **hunter clip** involving clipping the body out completely, except for a saddle patch and the legs, which gives warmth and protection to those areas. The jumping horse rarely requires his legs clipped right out, as in a **full clip**.

Clipping should be done by a professional if you have not done it before. There are many people who will come and do this with their own clippers and they usually advertise in the local papers on the equestrian pages or in tack shops or you may know of a friend who could do this for you. Find out their charge first and make sure the operators are capable; if possible, ask for a reference if you do not know them. At the time of writing, clipping charges range from £5 to £15 approximately, depending on the type of clip.

An electric power point will be necessary for the most usual type of clippers and somewhere safe and dry for the horse to stand. Most are clipped either in a stable, to prevent slipping should they move, or on a firm surface outside where the coat can easily be swept up. Obviously, as when dealing with anything electrical, everywhere should be dry and safe and, unless you are sure your horse or pony is completely happy about this procedure, it is a good idea to have an assistant to help. Hold the horse, especially when clipping sensitive areas like the head and between the legs. For a successful clip, the hair should be taken off in long, even sweeps against the lie of the coat, never up or down against it. The blades should be sharp so that they do not pull and snag, which could upset the horse as this will be most uncomfortable. Talk to him soothingly if he becomes a little nervous.

The stable

For those with their own stable, life is comparatively easy as you have everything to hand. The stable should be warm, dry and safe with good drainage. Make sure there are no electrical wires for the horse to take hold of nor switches that could be chewed or licked. Any sharp edges or protrusions should be padded or rounded off. There should be good ventilation and the door should be strong and secure. The minimum size of the stable should definitely be no smaller than 3 x 3 m (10 x 10 ft).

If you have a paddock, you will be able to turn your horse out daily, which is ideal, for no horse can really enjoy being confined to a box for around 23 hours a day. This also makes it very easy to muck out the bedding, and pile the clean bedding up at the sides to air it and to allow the floor to dry. The bed can then be put down in the evening before the horse comes in. Many horses do stay in, however, and are perfectly content as long as they get some exercise daily.

Various types of bedding can be used. Straw, shavings, sawdust, peat or paper are the most popular and preference depends very much on availability, cost and ease of disposal.

Water can be kept in buckets in a corner or set in rings clipped to the wall for those animals who enjoy knocking buckets over! Haynets should be tied to rings set high enough so that a horse cannot put a foot in the net when it is empty. Hayracks are ideal as long as they hold enough hay for the horse's requirements and the horse will not get an eyeful of 'bits' while eating.

The grass-kept horse

Many animals live out in the field and are still quite capable of competing although more time and effort are required to ensure that they are clean and tidy before riding.

The field must be securely fenced and safe, with no sharp edges or metal rubbish lying around on which the horse could get injured. It should have shelter and sufficient grazing and be rested for at least three months every year. If it is a small paddock, efforts should be made to pick up droppings daily, to help to prevent worm infestations, and the paddock should be topped (mown) where the grass has grown coarse and long as horses tend to ignore this. Sheep are excellent for eating up what horses leave and if it is possible to get them into your paddock for a time, to tidy it up and eat what the horses leave,

New Zealand rugs are a godsend in cold weather. Make sure you cross the leg straps to prevent soreness and chafing.

this will definitely be beneficial as will grazing cows if there is a lot of long grass. Cows and sheep are not hosts to the same varieties of worms as horses, therefore they are safe 'visitors'.

Check regularly to ensure that no poisonous plants are growing, such as ragwort, bracken or an excess of buttercups. Yew and ivy are poisonous, as are acorns which can cause severe colic. Most trees with berries are also poisonous to horses. If your paddock is adjacent to a road, check that bottles and cans have not been thrown over the fence and that the gate on to the road is kept padlocked. The theft of horses is on the increase and many people do not seem to realize how important it is to secure gates properly if they contain stock.

Check your horse's legs and feet regularly to ensure the shoes are secure and that mud fever is not developing nor

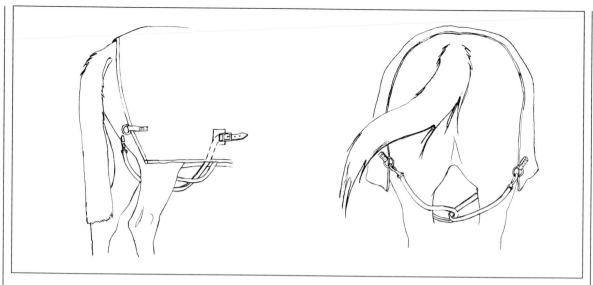

Two types of fastenings around the hind legs on a New Zealand rug. The straps must always be looped through one another or crossed as shown to prevent chafing on the insides of the legs.

any lumps or bumps. A little nick or sore can easily develop into a maddening infection if not treated early, which could prevent you competing when you want to. This can be very disappointing.

If your field does not have good shelter in the form of trees or a decent hedge, your horse will need either a New Zealand rug or a field shelter of some sort and will probably need the latter anyway if he is to remain out all winter. Make sure water is freely available, either from a trough or in a large tub that is topped up daily. If a stream runs through the field, check that it is unpolluted, safe and easy for the horse to drink from. If not, it should be fenced off to prevent an accident.

Tack for your horse

Tack must be safe, well fitting and suitable for what you want to do. In this case, you are specifically thinking about cross country, so control is vital and also extra equipment to ensure that the tack stays in place as well as giving adequate protection to the horse when jumping. The following items will provide a complete kit with which everyone should be able to compete.

The bridle

This must be well fitting, strong and comfortable for the horse. It should have at least one hole on either side by which the bit can be raised in the mouth should this be necessary or in case you decide to change the bit. If the bridle is too big, the horse can easily get his tongue over the bit causing great discomfort which can then be dangerous. The browband must be loose enough not to pinch the ears; the throatlatch should be long enough to ensure that you can place the width of your hand between it and the cheekbone when fastened.

Four main types of noseband can be used, in different ways, to help with steerage and control. The **flash** and **cavesson** are the only two to which a standing martingale can be fitted. The **grakle** helps to prevent a horse crossing his jaw, whereas the **drop** specifically helps to prevent the horse opening his mouth, as does the flash, and all will help by accentuating control.

Reins come in various different varieties but do make sure they are not too long and liable to hang down over your foot, which can easily become entangled in them. If they are long, always knot them up at the bottom. Choose a rein with a good grip – rubber-covered ones are popular as they do not slip if your hands are wet. Have a good look to see what sort you like and also check that their thickness is comfortable for your hands. Too thick or too narrow can be quite uncomfortably and make your hands ache.

The size of the bit must be right for your horse. If it is too narrow, it will pinch him and if too wide it will pull from side to side in his mouth, affecting its action and cause bruising and pain. Make sure you will have adequate control when you are galloping. It may not be necessary to have a stronger bit but, by adding a different noseband to prevent the horse from opening his mouth or crossing his jaw and perhaps a martingale to prevent the horse pulling downwards, you may find that you have all the extra control that is needed.

A kinder, more sensitive hand on the end of the rein is often more effective than endless yanking and pulling. However, if your horse is very unresponsive, something different must be tried, such as a Kimblewick or Pelham, perhaps with roundings, which still leaves you the option of riding with one rein. The shape of the horse's mouth and what he finds most comfortable are what is important. Some horses find the nutcracker action of the jointed snaffle too much but are quite happy in one, like a French link or Doctor Bristol, that has two links in the mouthpiece, the former being milder than the latter.

The saddle

Many people do not realize how important it is to purchase a saddle that allows them to adopt a comfortable and natural

Control is very important so try out different bits and nosebands to find the best for your particular horse. Some popular bits for cross country riding are shown here.

Vulcanite mullen mouthpiece

Doctor Bristol

Copper roller snaffle

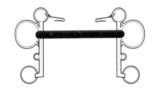

Pelham

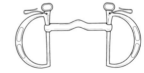

Kimblewick

Gag snaffle

37

position. You will need either a jumping or general-purpose saddle, which is less forward cut than the former. A very deep-seated saddle may feel comfortable to sit in but it is very unlikely that it will allow you enough freedom to change your position as you go over drop fences or when you want to move your weight back in the saddle to rebalance yourself for a combination of fences.

When trying a saddle, make sure you try it on the horse and are certain that it is the right fit for him as well as you. Saddles generally have three widths of tree and are more or less universally made nowadays with a spring tree to give greater comfort to the rider. Unfortunately, in many cases this has concentrated the rider's weight over one area, so it is important that you look for a saddle that spreads the weight over as wide an area as possible and allows you enough freedom, on a reasonably flat area, to adopt whatever position is necessary over your fences.

Most people spend quite a lot of money on saddles but a good one should last a lifetime if well cared for. They also have very good second-hand value and you may well find it worth while looking at these first as any good saddler usually has excellent second-hand saddles. Ask the saddler to check it over carefully to ensure that the girth straps and stitching, etc., are safe and secure. If you live close by and talk to him or her nicely, the saddler will usually come and see it fitted to your horse. All saddles require restuffing at times, so it may be necessary to get this done anyway with a second-hand saddle. New ones take time to wear in and may also require adjustments after you have had them a while. Watch carefully to ensure that they are not pressing down on to the withers or pinching on either side. There must always be a clear channel down the centre, to ensure that there is no pressure on the spine.

Girths must be safe and strong and not too long. As your horse becomes fitter, he will also become leaner, so choose girths that will not be too long when this happens. If well cared for, leather girths go on for a lifetime but they are expensive. If you choose one of the synthetic types, check that the stitching is strong and the buckles look robust. These girths are normally washable and will wear well but they do wear out over time. When this happens, they can rub the horse, so check them regularly.

Good irons and leathers are vital to your security. Rawhide leathers are the strongest and safest but can stretch a bit when new. Make sure that your irons are made of steel, not nickel

which snaps (the same goes for all metal, including bits and buckles). They must be wide enough to take your feet in riding boots with a quarter of an inch to spare on either side. Anything much smaller could mean your foot getting trapped should you have a fall.

Breastplates

A breastplate or breastgirth is designed to hold the saddle securely in position and stop it slipping back. This can easily happen with a fit horse that is on the lean side or when going up hills if the horse has done a bit of work and is sweaty and hot and the girths have slackened. Which type you use is purely a matter of choice but they must be well fitting to be effective and they are, I believe, an essential bit of kit for the serious competitor. The breastplate has the advantage of enabling you to use a martingale attachment should you need

This horse is wearing a breastgirth to prevent the saddle slipping back. She also has a running martingale and surcingle, passed through the martingale loop, to stop the saddle flaps rising and as an extra security strap.

one, rather than putting on a martingale as well as the breast-girth.

Surcingle

The surcingle or overgirth is designed to hold the saddle flaps in place and act as an extra security strap in the event of the girth breaking. If used, it must be secured by passing it through the loop or loops of the breastplate or girth, to prevent it from sliding back and becoming a bucking strap!

It is important that the buckle is fastened under the horse's belly where it cannot rub his elbows nor lie anywhere under your leg. While essential for racing and event riders and to hold weights in position, etc., I do not believe this to be such an important item for those doing hunter trials as long as their girths are safe and strong. If your saddle flaps are very soft, however, and tend to work up, then you should definitely use one and, anyway, they are not expensive. Get one with an elastic insert as these are easier to do up.

Martingales

Martingales are extremely useful for added control and steering. There are three main types, all having a different action: the **running**, **standing** and **Irish**. Correctly adjusted the running martingale helps with control and in turning, giving an accentuated action on the rein. It is vital that rein stops are used to prevent the rings of the martingale getting caught up

The running martingale is the most useful type. Correctly fitted, it helps with control and steering.

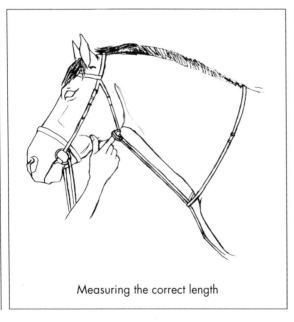

Measuring the correct length

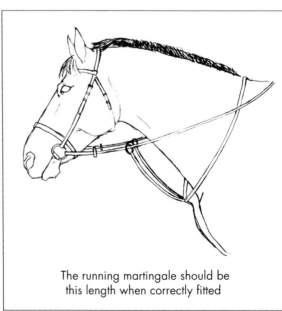

The running martingale should be this length when correctly fitted

on the buckles or billets of the rein where they attach to the bit. This could give a terrible jerk to the poor horse's mouth should they get caught up. The standing martingale is attached to the cavesson or top part of the flash noseband. This prevents the horse from raising his head out of the angle of control and is, I believe, an excellent gadget as it in no way interferes with the mouth.

The Irish martingale is a rather different idea altogether and is used to prevent the reins from separating and being tossed over the horses' head which can happen surprisingly easily with some animals who use their heads a lot at speed. It can also be used in conjunction with a running martingale, in the form of a bib martingale, which is a running martingale joined together at the top to prevent the rings separating by more than about 15 cm (6 in).

Boots and leg protection

Inevitably, when competing, there is a risk that injuries can occur and the horse's most vulnerable areas are his legs and

Boots should be protective, light and a good fit on the horse. If bandages are used they must be evenly and firmly applied and should not restrict the circulation between knee and fetlock joints.

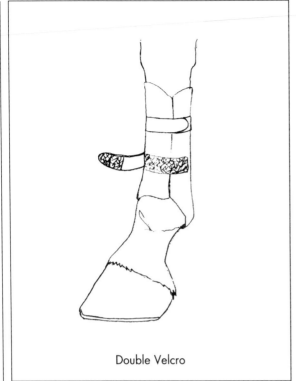

Double Velcro

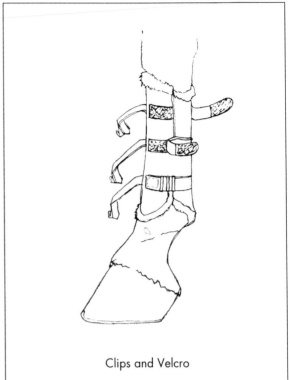

Clips and Velcro

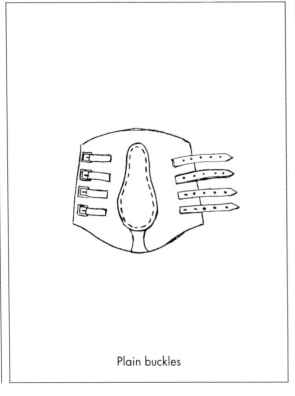

Plain buckles

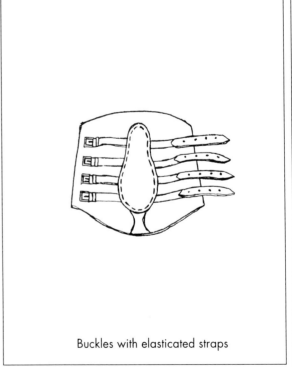

Buckles with elasticated straps

Left: Leg protection is most important to prevent bumps and bruises. Whether boots or bandages are used it is important to ensure that they fit snugly and do not in any way interfere with the horse's circulation.

Below: Overreach boots come in various designs and are used to protect the horse's front heels from the back hooves. The pull-on variety are pulled inside out, eased over the hoof and then turned back.

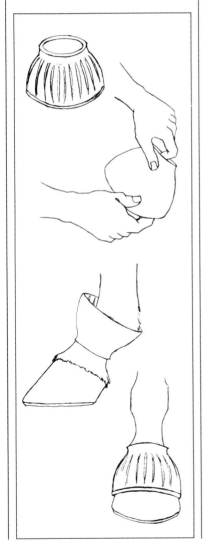

heels. To protect these, numerous varieties of boots, bandages and overreach boots are on the market. Generally, the simplest are often the best but the choice is endless.

Overreach boots must be of the right size for the horse to be effective. The rubber pull-on variety are excellent (those with buckles can get caught by the opposite foot) but they can be tough to pull on. Turn them inside-out to pull them on, then turn them down the right way.

If you use boots, remember what they are meant to be doing. They must protect the horse's legs without impeding his action or freedom. The vulnerable areas are the fronts and backs of the legs and, particularly, round the fetlock joints. They should be lightweight and safe when in place, so the fastenings must be good. Some boots rub the legs through the friction of movement and these minor injuries can be more troublesome than anything else. In good going, less rather than more can be a better idea. The front legs are more prone to injury than the back ones.

Alternatively, well-applied bandages over non-absorbent padding, or over leg shells, are good. The latter help to reduce the risk of overtightening a bandage round the leg, which can hinder circulation. The slightly sticky, elasticated bandages are excellent when used with these as they stick to themselves and so remove the danger of a bandage slipping down. Make sure they are well secured with tape as an extra precaution. Tape should never be pulled tighter than the original tension of the bandage round the leg.

Numnahs and saddlepads

Numnahs or saddlepads are designed to protect the horse's back from any rubs or soreness. These should not occur anyway if the saddle fits correctly and the rider sits centrally, however some modern saddles do place the rider's weight over a smaller area on the back, accentuating pressure on this part. Choose a good quality numnah or pad, the thin, limp variety rarely last for long, except for the strong cotton-linen ones. The pad or numnah must be slightly larger than your saddle, to ensure that the edges are not exactly under the very place you are trying to protect.

Try to look the part with your horse's tack. The real professionals stick to plainer colours, so choose tack that is neutral, if possible, with brown, black or blue pads and girths, etc. Keep white ones for shows if you wish. Bright reds, pinks or multicolours are a bit over the top, except for team colours for chases, etc.

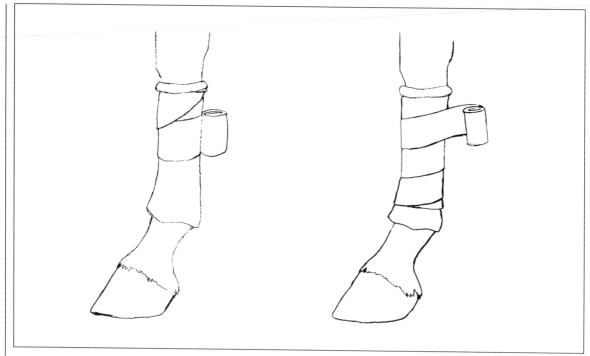

The rider's equipment

The rider must also have the necessary equipment. As a rider, you will already probably have breeches and boots (or jodhpurs and jodhpur boots for children) and should have a skull cap with a harness, conforming to recognized safety standards, which is compulsory for most events. Many riders now use back protectors, of which the waistcoat variety is the most comfortable and popular. If you do not have one, this is the first thing to go out and buy as more and more jumping competitions are now making them compulsory. I have thanked mine on numerous occasions when it has saved me from bumps and bruises.

Gloves are another essential. What sort is a matter of preference but string or 'pimple' gloves are ideal as they do not slip when your horse's neck becomes sweaty and wet, affecting your grip on the reins.

A stock (hunting tie) should always be worn when riding across country as it supports the neck and also protects it from scratches from branches etc. when galloping through woods. A coloured stock is the most useful as it is fine with your cross country colours and is correct with a tweed coat, traditionally worn at hunter trials. (White or pale cream is worn with a blue or black hunting coat only. These are not worn at hunter

Above: Exercise bandages provide extra support, especially when competing.

Right: Preparing the rider's and the horse's equipment for a competition requires careful planning to ensure that nothing is forgotten.

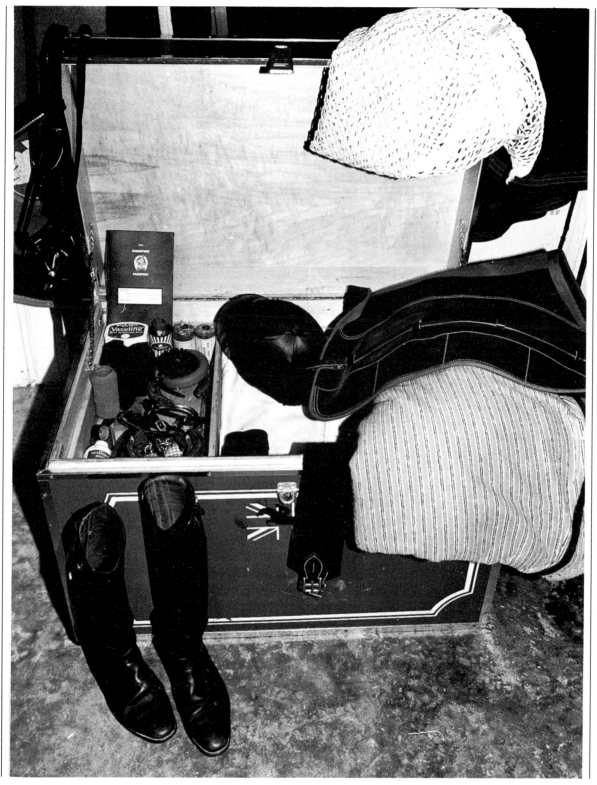

Spurs should be properly fitted, with the shank at the back pointing downwards. Do not have too long a shank unless you have a sluggish horse.

trials where tweed coats are correct and cross country colours are now becoming acceptable.)

Spurs should be worn with hunting boots but choose a pair that are not too long unless you have a particularly sluggish horse; 1.25 – 1.8 cm (½–¾in) is quite long enough in most cases. The buckle on the strap should do up on the outside, with the end pointing downwards. The shank at the back must always turn down – nothing looks sillier than a rider with their spurs on upside down!

Whips are a vital aid and should be strong with a rounded top so that it will not be too painful if it pokes in your eye! Some people like those with a large top, others wrap a few elastic bands around the hand area to prevent the stick slipping through their hand. Generally, most whips used for jumping do not exceed 76 cm (30 in) in length.

CHAPTER 2

TRAINING

Training the horse for competition is a challenge and, if done well, is extremely rewarding and satisfying. To be successful the horse must first be fit enough to cope with the demands made of him and then made capable of meeting those demands through training.

Some horses are naturally bold and good at jumping, taking on whatever they are aimed at, within reason, as long as they are not overfaced with too big a fence until they have sufficient experience and confidence to be able to jump it. Others require more time and help with the basics and must be taught

Early roadwork is important to harden up legs and tendons. This rider is leading one horse to save time.

After a period of slow work to harden up tendons and muscles the training programme should be gradually increased week by week. Cantering up hills gently is quite strenuous and should not be overdone.

how to improve their technique and so make it easy for them to build up their confidence and ability.

Fitness

The fitness of the horse must first be worked on, so that tendons and muscles are well toned-up and the lungs will start to expand more and become efficient enough to cope with heavier exertion. If the horse has not been worked at all, a programme must be arranged to ensure a gradual build-up of work. How this is done rather depends on whether you will be riding him from the field or whether he is stabled all the time or just in at night and out by day. Many people do the opposite in the heat of the summer, turning their horses out when it is cooler and bringing them in away from the heat and flies during the day.

For any horse, a two-week period at least must be set aside for slow work to start with if he really has had a long break, while grass-kept horses will need a little longer. If he has not had very long off, then this could be changed to one week's walking, half an hour to start, working up to a good hour by the end of the first week. The second week could then go from one hour's walking to one and a half hours of walk and slow trotting by the end of this time. The next two weeks can be a bit more energetic, with more trotting and a bit of steady cantering at the end of the third to fourth week. Let the horse tell you how he is feeling. If he feels tired with what you are doing, back off a bit; if rather fresh, then do a little more but avoid long periods at faster paces. Make haste slowly at this stage.

If, for any reason, you are unable to use the roads or have no suitable firm tracks, then you can work your horse in a field or

You can vary your rides out to incorporate a few streams which will help when it comes to cross country practice. Note the thick pad under the saddle to help distribute the rider's weight. This is especially important when the horse is only walking.

49

school. The reason why the road is so good to start off with is that it is consistently firm and gives the horse an even surface to work on that will not give way nor produce uneven patches that could cause strain or injury to soft tendons and muscles.

If using the field or a school, avoid working on too small a circle to start with and trot for short periods frequently, rather than for a long time all in one go. Avoid deep going, if possible, for the first couple of weeks. During this time, make your horse walk on energetically and start your trotting a little earlier as he is likely to get bored and may become a bit silly if kept walking in the same place for too long. Gradually increase your work week by week.

When doing your slow work, try to alter your position in the saddle so that you do not sit on the same spot continuously without moving, which could result in a sore back. Use a good numnah under your saddle when doing slow work, to relieve the pressure on the back which will be soft anyway after a lay-off.

Watch your horse's condition. If he is very fat, you will need to cut his food down considerably over a period of time. You do not want to go galloping on a fat horse as this will put strain on his heart and lungs and increase the risk of tendon strain in his legs.

The leaner horse may also need adjustment in his feeding routine by adding a few more fattening foods such as sugar-beet, a fattening mix or barley. Check that he has been wormed and his teeth are in good shape. If he sweats a lot, decide on an appropriate clip to help to prevent weight loss.

Once the horse has done two to four weeks of slow, steady work out hacking, ideally on the roads or firm tracks if those are available to you, you can start to do some schooling.

Early flatwork

Begin on the flat to ensure that he is obedient and listens to your demands - turns evenly in either direction, goes straight and moves forwards directly from your leg. All this is very important if he is to be a really good ride across country. Suppling exercises will help enormously and will ensure that your horse will be able to take the fastest route when galloping as he will respond easily to your demands. So often, both in show jumping and across country, you can see seconds being wasted as a rider tugs away, trying to turn a stiff or unresponsive horse.

Right: **There are numerous exercises that can be done to loosen and supple your horse. Also always include circles of various sizes on both reins.**

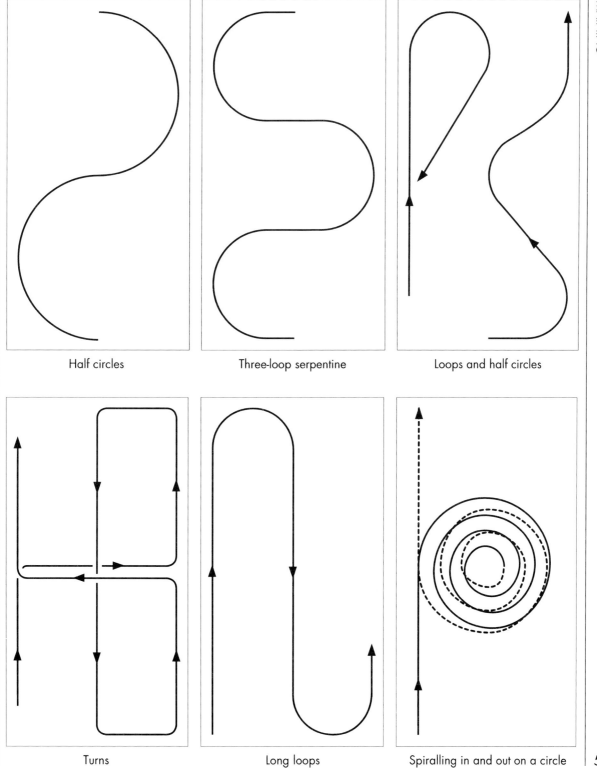

Half circles

Three-loop serpentine

Loops and half circles

Turns

Long loops

Spiralling in and out on a circle

Many suppling exercises are done using poles or, as in this case, as preparation for jumping grids of fences.

Numerous exercises can be used to help your horse to find turns and bends easy to cope with. They will also help you to sharpen up your co-ordination. Until they have ridden, few people realize how difficult it is to use legs and hands to do different things at the same time!

Many of the exercises can be done over trotting poles, which will increase the effort the horse has to make and so make him work a little harder. Others can be done round and through the poles. It is very satisfying to feel how your horse improves as he loosens up and finds the work a little easier day by day. Be careful not to overdo such work as it is quite strenuous. Ten to fifteen minutes is ample with work of this sort. To start with, you only want to get the horse used to what you are asking and to respond with ease.

The rider must be very conscious of staying straight at all times, with their weight evenly spread through the seatbones and on into the lower leg. The ankle joint should be flexible, with the weight going still further down in to the heel.

Once the horse finds the flatwork easy and is coping well with your fitness hacks, you can start to think about jumping. Anyone with a reasonably bold horse can go and jump a series of straightforward fences but you need to be preparing your horse for the more difficult aspects at this stage of training, so that when you do come across something more complicated, you will know exactly how to tackle it.

Early jump training

For your jump training, it is an excellent idea to do a little work over grids. This involves jumping a series of poles on the ground, and also small fences, and it teaches your horse to shorten or lengthen his stride and shift his weight to cope with the different demands. It also helps him to judge the correct take-off point.

It is important to start with a simple grid consisting of a pole on the ground, followed by a simple cross pole and

A little grid work will help the horse to be more observant and foot-perfect over the fences. It will also assist the horse and rider balance.

A simple grid

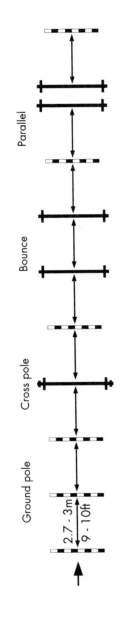

Ground pole | Cross pole | Bounce | Parallel

2.7 - 3m / 9 - 10ft

Practising uprights and spreads

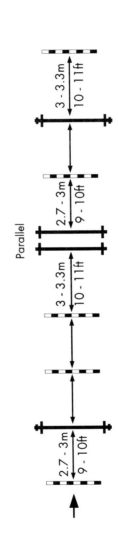

Parallel

2.7 - 3m / 9 - 10ft

3 - 3.3m / 10 - 11ft

2.7 - 3m / 9 - 10ft

3 - 3.3m / 10 - 11ft

A more demanding grid

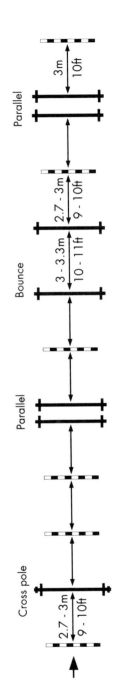

Cross pole | Parallel | Bounce | Parallel

2.7 - 3m / 9 - 10ft

3 - 3.3m / 10 - 11ft

2.7 - 3m / 9 - 10ft

3m / 10ft

Left: **Examples of grids used to teach the horse to shorten and lengthen his stride. Sit up over the ground poles and go forwards over the fences. The distances between elements must be altered to suit your horse's stride.**

perhaps a pole on the ground a stride away, followed by another small fence a stride away after that. Thereafter, you can add fences, but do make sure that you set your fences at the right distances, otherwise it will do more harm than good. All horses have slightly different strides, some taking short ones, others long, but if you place the poles and jumps at approximately 3 m (10 ft) distance apart from each other you will be fairly safe. Obviously, for ponies they will need to be closer.

It may not be possible to do grids for one reason or another, so then you should practise over single fences once or twice a week if possible. These can be made up using barrels or drums with poles on them if you have nothing else. Straw bales can also be used. Always put something behind drums to prevent them rolling in the wind or if you knock them, as they can be dangerous if not secure.

Work on turning into a fence or changing direction immediately after it. Also put up two fences close together as a double or even three as a treble, to accustom your horse to such combinations. It is important to try to get the distances right for a comfortable jump for your horse. As a general rule, if you take eight normal walking strides from the back of one fence to the front of the next, this will give your horse room for one non-jumping stride in between the two fences. Twelve normal walking strides will give approximately two non-jumping strides in between. (This is based on an average sized adult's normal walking stride of about 90 cm (3 ft).

If you do not have access to an arena or area where you can use some jumps, you may find some fences when out hacking, in the form of logs and small ditches. These can often be very useful introductions to cross country fences; gorse bushes are sometimes a good shape and, being rather spiky, horses tend to respect them and jump them well. With all fences, check that the landings are safe before jumping.

Water training

Water often seems a little daunting, especially to young horses, so the more puddles and streams you can go through to get the horse accustomed to this, the better. Ensure that it is safe before going through rivers or deep water: nothing puts a horse off quicker than suddenly to find itself floundering on what appears to be a very insecure surface. Some horses are so frightened that they never get over this and will not go into water again. Always remember that a horse needs confidence

and will only acquire this if we never put him in a position of losing faith in us – or, at least, try not to do so too often!

If the horse is rather nervous of water, ask a friend to come along with you as horses will usually follow one another and, once he has been into the water a few times, he will normally go again on his own. Patience and firmness are often required.

Control

If you live near a wooded area and are lucky enough to have good, wide tracks, it is worth practising cantering along, keeping the horse sufficiently under control to weave in and out of the trees. If you have worked your horse well on the flat, he should be nice and supple and find this easy. A stiff horse will not, however, and it may well be your knees that suffer.

Another exercise that can, and should, be practised, either when schooling or out hacking, is one to help you to control your pace and speed coming into a fence.

Shorten and lengthen your stride at trot and canter by increasing and decreasing the pace regularly. Riding across country is not only about speed but also about control and balance on approaching the fence. If your horse listens to you, he should respond when you ask him to steady a little or push on into a fence. There is nothing worse than riding a horse that does not respond to you and, in some cases, this can even become quite frightening, particularly if you find yourself galloping downhill with a rather daunting obstacle at the bottom. This type of fence needs a steady, controlled approach!

As your horse gets fitter, he may also become stronger, so be ready to adjust your breaking system if you are not able to keep the horse sufficiently under control. He is likely to be worse in a competition, so you want to be quite certain you can at least manage him safely at home.

To adjust your pace, you should practise sitting up against your horse a little, by closing your legs and asking him to steady with your hands. This should not be a continuous tug but a soft take and give, take and give action, until he responds, which should be fairly instantaneous if he is obedient. At canter, you will need to prevent him from breaking back into a trot by keeping your leg on and asking him to shorten his stride rather than necessarily going a lot slower.

This exercise can take quite a lot of patience to perfect but will make a lot of difference to how well you will be able to ride your fences, whether they are of cross country or show

This rider looks nicely under control. The horse is wearing a gag snaffle which can aid control if the horse is strong.

jumping design. Once you can do this well at a strong canter, increase the pace to a slow gallop and then ask you horse to steady for you. Remember, everything must be gradual but you should get some effect immediately to feel safe and in charge of your horse.

Sponsored rides

By the time you have done all this and your horse has been working for five to eight weeks, he should be ready to do some type of competition. One way of just testing that everything is coming on well, without putting yourself under any particular strain, is by doing a fun or sponsored ride. Most have optional fences but a few do not. Choose one that does, if possible, as this is a great way of going out among everyone, seeing how your horse reacts with others and getting yourself into the swing of competing. You can jump as many or as few of the fences as you like and if you join up with a couple of friends this can be most enjoyable, providing, of course, the weather is right!

The UK Chasers provide a series of courses, spread over

8– 9 km (5 – 6 miles), and dotted throughout the UK, which you can go to practise over every weekend. It is worth checking to see if one is located near you as they are all well built and, again, the fences are varied in size for you to take your choice. Sometimes there are special rides over these in aid of local charities, so that everyone helps everyone else in some way, and you and your horse can decide whether or not you are set to stun the world once you have jumped all the fences.

Hunting

Hunting is probably the very best possible way to learn all about cross country as you have no idea where you are going, what you will jump or what will happen from one minute to the next. The ground is also very variable as, of course, is the weather, so you and the horse are constantly adapting to unknown situations and, without being aware of it, are building up that all-important partnership that comes through mutual confidence.

If you are having any problems at the beginning of the season, it is almost a certainty that, if you have really set out to go well in the hunting field, you will be a star performer by the end and, of course, horses love being in a crowd.

Drag hunting is also very popular and has the advantage that you know where you are going to start and finish and also when, which can be a great blessing to those who are short of time.

To go hunting or drag hunting, you need to get in touch with the hunt secretary to find out whether they allow visitors and when. You may wish to be a subscriber, which is expensive depending on the hunt, or just go in the cubbing season, which normally involves special rates or, in some cases, no charge at all. Pony Club members are given special rates and most hunts have a special children's meet during school holidays. Every hunt has its own special rules and regulations and the sport is controlled by the Masters of Foxhounds Association.

Team chases

The team chase is another type of event that is becoming more and more popular these days. It consists of teams of three to four riders going round a hunter trial type of course together. The best team member going clear, or the fastest three members over a certain part or timed section of the course,

Above: Team chases are great fun and help to get horse and rider going forwards. Some fences need to be jumped abreast. These three are doing well as they are all over the fence together.

Left: For pairs classes you need to practise riding together and keeping straight. Plan which side you are going to ride over each fence and stick to it.

determines the time for that team. The fastest team or the team nearest the bogey time is the winner. There may be certain fences over which you are required to jump together as a team, known as 'dressing' fences.

The courses vary from small, over which the 'fun competition' or Cubhunters or Novice class is run, to the open class, which is usually quite large, with fences of anything up to 114 cm (3 ft 9 in).

This can be tremendous fun, especially if you go with friends and you decide who is to be the leader round the course. This should be a confident rider on a bold horse. The rest of the team must try to stay close up behind, with the back marker also being well briefed to look after the two middle members should anything happen. You need to have a plan of action should someone not go well and either tell them to give up and walk quietly home or, if they are just having the odd stop, be ready to give a lead as you approach the fence if the first two have gone on ahead and have yet to realize you are not all up together. To look good, you should all dress the same in your 'team colours'.

Pairs classes

Team chases often have a pairs class to start the day off, as do many hunter trials at all levels. These are, perhaps, the most useful training classes of all as a certain amount of skill is required to jump together as a pair anyway and, with two, you can help each other along and issue instruction as you do so as to who should be helping whom if one horse is a bit unsure of himself. To jump together safely, you must both keep straight and stay on the same side of the fence even if you are not always together. Decide first of all who is going to stay on the right or left and then aim at that side of the centre of each fence so that you allow your partner enough room.

Some horses tend to speed up a little when jumping with another horse, so keep your pace consistent and do not allow yourselves to get out of control. Giving it confidence beside a companion is a great way of helping a young horse to get going. Practise jumping together as often as you can and work on staying together as a pair. This will help you to be more effective as well as teaching the horse to be responsive to your aids and more obedient. Having jumped all the fences in the pairs class, you can often go in the next class of a hunter trial on your own to see how your horse gets on.

Hunter trials

The purpose of this book is to give guidance on riding in a hunter trial and if you have had the chance to do some or all of the previous activities you and your horse are more than likely ready to go out and have a lot of fun at a hunter trial.

Timed sections

If the course includes a timed section, this may include just a gate, should there be one, or it may be over two or three fences and it is important to know where this starts and finishes. There will usually be a notice outside the secretary's tent telling you where it is and how it is to be judged. It will usually also be marked on the course by either flags or posts, etc. Find out if the winner is the fastest time to complete this or the nearest to the bogey time. If the former, then you know you have to speed up over that part of the course but if it is to be judged by bogey time, this is not usually announced until the end, so you are kept guessing!

Gates

There are certain specific things that you need to practise and the most common of these is having to open and shut a gate! This may sound simple but to bring your horse back to a halt and then open a gate, when he has been galloping across country, can be a bit of a problem as he will be quite fidgety and liable to move just as you have got yourself in position to open the gate.

The gates tend to be specially erected in the middle of a field in most cases, so they look totally out of place for a start! There may be two, side by side, if this obstacle is also used in the pair class. Some have an easy opening, with just a chain to lift off and put back on, others are not so simple. It may be easier to get off, lead through and then get on again if your horse is fairly small and you are feeling particularly agile and confident about getting on again! This does not normally penalize you but check first if you think there is any chance of this particular competition being different.

Opening a gate

Although in a competition you will have to adapt to the gate of the day, it is as well to know now how a gate should be opened as this is rarely explained in books. To be easy, it requires a certain degree of obedience from the horse. You should ride your horse up parallel with the gate with the

Teaching a horse to walk up to and stand quietly beside a gate while you open it is excellent training for any young horse. It will also stand you in good stead when competing in hunter trials where quick gate-opening is one of the assets of a good competitor.

horse's head stopping just past the catch. Take both reins and whip in the outside hand and, with your free, inside hand, undo the catch. (This is where problems sometimes occur when you discover the gate to be immovable!) Once undone, push the gate open and walk your horse through, turning him round as you do so, and then push the gate closed, either with your hand or by asking your horse with your outside leg to nudge it gently closed. Halt him beside the catch, fasten the gate and then away you go!

It may all sound very easy, and would be if your horse was obedient to the leg, stood still when you leant over or down to open and shut it or if the gate is well hung in the first place. However, to find all three happening as they should is, unfortunately, a rarity, so it is worth spending a little time practising at home if you can find a good gate on which to do this. Teach your horse to stand quietly alongside a gate to start with. So often they fidget around but practice does (usually) make perfect and it is certainly worth it in the end to have a horse standing quietly and allowing you to get on with the business of opening and shutting.

Sometimes you may have to let down a slip rail, which is relatively simple. Again, bring your horse alongside the rail, slide it back and let it drop, then walk over the end. This is not often encountered nowadays as so many rails tend to get broken!

Pens, etc.

Some fences include a type of pen (which will be discussed fully in Chapter 3). This may involve a straightforward in-and-out which is enclosed by rails, or involve jumping in and then turning to jump out at right angles. It is at this sort of fence that the obedience of the horse becomes so important.

Occasionally, such a combination exists for use in the pairs classes or even for teams, the rules stating that both members of the pair must be in the pen before they jump out, or that three members of the team must be in the pen before the leader is allowed to jump out! All these little ideas stem from the original theory that hunter trials were the training grounds for good all-round hunters. Nowadays, they are still excellent training grounds for everything and anything.

Remember that some horses become excited in restricted spaces, so, if you do have to wait in a confined space, it is as well to keep the horses walking round quietly until you can move on again should you have to wait for your partner or team mates.

Hacks out in the countryside and riding through water will help to train the horse to be confident.

Left: Whoops! Sometimes things go wrong but practice makes perfect if you keep trying.

Below: This rider is entering the timed section of the course. The fastest clear round over this part is likely to win.

Top left: Taking it steady over this rail and ditch will allow the horse time to work out what is expected of him.

Bottom left: Hunting is fun and one of the best training grounds for competition horses.

Below: A run out like this will incur 20 penalties. Three run outs will mean elimination.

This combination looks very happy, but would lose marks for not being quite together as a pair if they were jumping a dressing fence.

Riding clubs and Pony Club

If you do not already belong, it may be fun to join a local riding club which caters for all and can help with training in all aspects of riding and jumping. For children, the Pony Club is tremendous fun, with endless activities covering everything and hunter trials usually arranged in the holidays for all age groups. Activities are usually advertised in the local papers, saddlery shops and riding schools.

It is always fun if you can do various activities with friends as you can help one another so much and give encouragement and advice. It is often much easier to see from the ground what is required rather than feeling it from on top.

There is so much to learn in riding and how far you want to go varies from one individual to another but the more you want to learn the bigger the subject becomes. Anyone can sit on a horse and go hacking and even, after some practice, jump fences (some more easily than others as this very much depends on co-ordination, balance and natural ability).

Improving the rider

Once you have mastered the basic skills of riding and jumping, it is worth considering how to improve and understand why certain things do or do not happen. The rider's position is vital to future progress and perhaps now is the time to check this to ensure bad habits are not developing and that the correct aids are being given to the horse.

In some cases, certain horses are not necessarily very well schooled in the true sense of the words but do everything asked by the rider. The phrase 'on the bit' does not mean much to many riders and probably even less to the horse. In fact, many people think of such terms as meaning something to do with 'dressage' which they do not understand. This is not the case; at the end of it, it boils down to the obedience of the horse to the rider's instructions (aids).

Position in the saddle

To be effective the rider's position must be natural, straight, relaxed and comfortable but not in any way slouched or floppy. You should be able to feel both seatbones equally if you are sitting straight and this is one thing to be constantly aware of. Feel the same weight on each foot in the stirrup irons, also making sure that these are even in the first place. Your weight should be pushed down the leg into the heel with the ankle

These two pictures show the basic positions in the saddle for galloping and jumping or for sitting upright. The stirrups should always be shortened for galloping, when your seat comes out of the saddle, otherwise you will be reaching down for them and will lose the vital security of your lower leg.

and knee joints acting as shock absorbers. The toe should rest lightly in the iron but not push as this would raise the heel. The heel should always remain the lowest point when riding and jumping. The legs are your anchor and should be close to the horse but relaxed at all times. If these are firm, still and secure, you will find it fairly easy to sit up straight and proud in the saddle and remain balanced above your horse.

The lower leg is vital to your security. If you are sitting upright and balanced, there should be a perpendicular line from your shoulder through your hip to your heel. Your head must be upright and looking ahead, never poked forwards, spoiling both the balance (as the head is remarkably heavy) and the overall picture. The shoulders should be erect but not stiff or rounded. The back must be upright, with the weight evenly distributed on both seatbones. It must not be hollowed or slouched in the saddle – two faults very commonly seen.

The legs must hang down naturally and softly on either side of the horse, as must the arms by the rider's sides, with a relaxed, bent elbow joint. The hands should close safely round the reins and be held just above the withers. The fingers and wrists should be able to 'give' forwards as necessary, following the movement of the horse's head without interrupting the arm position. The palms should turn in naturally towards one another with the fingers closed round the reins. The rein is normally held between the fourth and little finger and comes up across the palm and out between the first finger and thumb. Perhaps the best way to describe the type of contact is to imagine you hold the reins as you would a sponge – firm but not tight.

The above deals with the basic position when standing still but this has to adapt to the action of the horse as he moves in the different paces or over a fence. The rider has to keep in balance with the horse at all times and this is achieved through contact with the legs, seat and hands and the ability to work forward with the horse rather than come back against him. The closer the seat and legs are to the horse, the easier this is to achieve.

Position at the different paces

The position of the rider has to adapt slightly with each different pace, to ensure that the forward momentum and balance are not lost. At walk, which is a pace with a four-time beat, there is quite a nodding of the horse's head as he lifts up each leg to move forward. The rider must therefore allow the hands to travel with this movement, otherwise they will be restricting the forwardness of the horse, taking hold on each alternate step and losing it when the opposite two steps are taken.

In trot, the pace is, or should be, a rhythmic two-time beat, with a moment of suspension as the horse changes from one diagonal to the other. It can be ridden either rising or sitting. With some horses, it is quite difficult to maintain good balance if the horse has quite a springy trot and the rider sometimes resorts to maintaining balance through the hands rather than the legs and seat. It is important to find your point of balance and maintain this through your position in the saddle. If you lean back too much you could get behind the movement, whereas tipping forward could mean you get in front of the horse. The hands must not be used as a balancing aid and should remain independent. It is easy to push them down into the wither so that they become fixed, or carry them too high so that you lose balance and interfere with the horse's mouth. You need to maintain the up-down rhythm, along with the forward movement, when in rising trot. For sitting trot, you must relax your back and stay in forward balance with the movement of the horse. Do a little at a time.

In canter, which is a three-beat pace, incorporating a moment of suspension, there is also a slight elevation as the horse lifts three feet off the ground for a split second and propels forward to the next stride. The rider must absorb the movement of the horse through their lower back and legs and maintain an erect upper body. The line from the shoulder through the hip to the heel must remain constant, with the weight kept evenly on both seatbones. It is in canter and gallop that the jumping rider takes most fences, so it is very important for all riders to feel secure in these paces before they tackle fences. A slightly forward seat is usually adopted in canter before a fence.

Position for galloping and jumping

For galloping and jumping, the leathers should be shortened so that there is greater leverage to help with the control of the horse and your own balance. By increasing the angle between hip, knee and ankle, it becomes easier to balance oneself in the forward seat, which should feel more secure as you are closer to the centre of gravity.

The reins are shortened and the hands are carried lower and further forward up the neck, with the body tilted forward. The shoulders come down and the hips go back a little as the seat becomes lighter in the saddle. It is vital at this point that the rider finds and maintains a comfortable balanced position, following the movement of the horse.

It will take a bit of practice in this position to feel really safe and secure and to be able to maintain balance through the legs and hands, as well as the seat which all ultimately work together to control the horse, ready for whatever is in store. This may include going up or down hills, through deep or slippery ground, over rough terrain or, of course, over a fence. There may need to be an adjustment to your pace as you prepare for the fence but the less you change your position the better, except to sit up a bit more to change the balance as necessary.

The less adjustment you make in front of the fence, the better the horse will be able to concentrate on his jump. The rider should keep the horse in a well-balanced stride, adjusting the approach, if necessary, with barely perceptible balancing between the arms and the legs. Tugging and pulling of any

Correct position is vital. This rider is insecure because his lower leg has come back and he is using his hands for support, but he has given the horse enough freedom.

kind will only result in the horse tensing his muscles and tightening, which prevents a really successful jump. The less you do as the rider, the more the horse is able to do with his jump, as long as you stay in balance with him.

It is important, however, to make adjustments in pace in time to ensure a safe jump. Galloping fast downhill towards an upright fence at the bottom is a recipe for disaster. The horse must be steadier early on and kept in a safe, steady canter for such a fence. Likewise, when going uphill to a fence, it is equally important that you help the horse here by pushing him forward into the bridle to be able to make the effort required for an uphill jump.

If your horse is very strong, it may be that you need to shorten your leathers to enable you to sit up against him a little more. This should give you more security in your leg, although you will often have to experiment a bit to find what is comfortable. What may seem very short when you are sitting upright on the horse is not necessarily the case when you get forward with your seat slightly back and just off the saddle in the galloping position. The reins will also need to be considerably shorter. If the leathers are too short, you will tend to lose the effectiveness of your legs. If the reins are too long, you will not be able to gain maximum control. Always put a knot in the end if they are long so that they do not become looped round your foot. Think of a change of bit if the horse feels in any way out of control.

To discover whether you can control your horse or not will require quite a lot of work in canter as you work on his fitness and this will also help you considerably with your own fitness which is just as important as that of the horse. Try cantering both with your seat in the saddle and then in jumping position. Remember that your heel must be the lowest point, absorbing the movement down through the leg. Make your horse settle into a good rhythm and see if you can maintain this without being pulled unduly. Practise on both reins and then be sure you can pull him up quite easily.

Cantering is one of the main ways of fittening your horse once you have done the initial, slow leg work and it will help to clear his wind which may be a little thick until you have done a bit of faster work. It will also help to get you fit for riding, which is equally important if you are to continue to enjoy riding without suffering unduly from stiffness.

Rider fitness

The fitness of the rider is one of the most important aspects to be considered, along with that of the horse. To be able to manage and care for the animal, you need to be quite fit anyway and to ride every day is definitely one of the best ways of getting yourself in shape. If this is possible, remember that slopping along will not help you or your horse. You must make a conscious effort to make your horse march forward into the bridle so that he is working his muscles and you are working yours fairly energetically. The lazy horse will need pushing anyway, so you will have to work hard. The energetic one will be nice and free-going but you will have to work in a different way to restrain him at times and his quicker movement will ensure that your body is moving faster to match his.

If you are not able to ride every day but only, perhaps, at weekends, you may need to take extra exercise to ensure that you are able to cope without becoming tired or stiff. For riding, you need to build up your leg and back muscles and there are few better ways of doing this than walking, jogging and bicycling. Swimming is also excellent, as is dancing, aerobics and any of the general exercise routines that encourage you to build up gradually on a fitness programme.

If you are starting from scratch, remember that the same principles apply to you as to your horse. You must build up your exercise gradually, never do anything to excess and be conscientious about how often you practise. It is not necessary to exercise seriously every day but something like three to four times a week will ensure that you build up to a certain level of fitness. Many people make a concerted effort to start with, then lose heart or get bored, but if you work out a routine that suits you, most people can manage to do some useful fitness work fairly frequently.

Walking upstairs, rather than using a lift, is beneficial and is certainly quite strenuous if there are several flights to cope with. Start with a few and then increase each time if this is possible. Alternatively, you can increase your speed as you go up them and it will not be long before you find that what was once a bit of an effort at walk becomes quite easy at a run after a bit of practice!

I was in the middle of my nursing training when I was selected to ride in the Olympic Three-Day Event and, although nursing involves quite a lot of walking and exercise generally, I had to think seriously of ways to keep myself in peak fitness while being unable to ride more than three to four times a week. Stairs certainly played a major role and going up six flights, up to ten times a day, was particularly helpful. You do not, however, need to be that energetic for hunter trials.

Swimming is very good too, as you have to learn to breathe properly if you are going to be able to perform for any length of time and this is one problem many riders find difficult to master early on. It is easy to get into the habit of holding one's breath, instead of breathing normally, when concentrating on something like riding but it is vital to overcome this if you want to get anywhere. Singing or talking to yourself can help while you are riding. You can recite rhymes to each other if you are riding with a friend – anything to ensure that you breathe properly!

Skipping is another good form of exercise, which will help fitness and also helps to loosen ankles and wrists. I gradually worked up to doing around one thousand a day but two to three hundred would probably be a good level to work up to – three to four times a week.

Degrees of fitness vary tremendously from person to person and are affected by their lifestyle and body metabolism – some may need to work really hard on their fitness, while others seem to need to do very little. As long as you are in shape to be able to hold your horse together and stay in balance with him round a course of fences of the length likely to be met in your competitions, you are probably fit enough for what you want to do. If you find yourself tiring, then you must do something about it before you or your horse injure yourselves, which easily happens if this aspect of riding is not taken seriously enough.

Here the rider is suffering the consequences of too long a stirrup and has resorted to the reins for security as the horse prepares for take off. The heel is starting to come up.

Riding exercises to help fitness

While riding every day helps to get you fit in the first place, it is when riding at speed and galloping and jumping that fitness really tells. Often you will find that your thighs and calves ache, as well as your back, when you have been galloping. Unless your horse is very strong, this should not be the case if you are fit enough.

First decide if you are riding short enough for this pace. Being out of the saddle, you will need to shorten your stirrups at least two or three holes on either side when galloping and jumping. If you are riding too long, you will be reaching down for your irons all the time, which is tiring and will encourage you to bring your heel up, losing security. Riding too long will also mean that you are balancing more on your thighs and knees, gripping upwards, rather than firmly down in the saddle.

As you ride shorter, you should feel yourself able to put more weight down into your heel. Practise cantering with your seat out of the saddle, thinking all the time of 'weight

This rider has a shorter and, therefore, more secure lower leg. She is going to be more able to stay in balance with her horse as she goes over the fence.

into heel' and staying in balance with your horse. Once you can do this comfortably for three to four minutes, try a more difficult variation of taking your hands away from the neck. This will help to ensure that you are not using your hands to balance yourself. It will also help you to realize how important it is to stay in balance with your horse and how much we all rely on our hands to do this. If you are firm in your seat and leg, you will not find this too difficult but, if not, it will really make you sort yourself out!

Sitting trot without stirrups is the classic way of improving your riding but do ensure you are sitting correctly and not getting into bad habits. You do need an instructor to keep you in the right position. You can, however, practise by yourself in trot and cantering by remembering the importance of

Riding without stirrups is an excellent way of improving your position in the saddle and developing general riding fitness.

sitting straight, letting your legs become as long as possible and not slouching your upper body but following your horse's movement with a supple lower back and upright top half.

When changing from one pace to another, consciously think about staying with your horse and do not let your legs or body swing too far back or forwards as the horse changes from one pace to another. It is so easy to let yourself get into bad habits that you need to be quite sure in your own mind where you should be as the horse does different things – in general, you should be straight, with an even contact on the reins and with your legs evenly applied to the horse's sides.

Riding up and down hills

Cantering up and down hills requires a certain balance from both horse and rider. If there are some hills near you, that are not too steep, both you and the horse will benefit from practising going up and down in both trot and canter. Quite a lot of impulsion is required when trotting up hills, so the rider should stay forward with a light seat and support, but not restrict, the horse's head. The legs should be on, urging the horse gently forward. On rougher ground the rider will need to maintain a rather stronger feel on the reins than when trotting on the roads, for instance.

To come down hills, you must remain in balance with your horse, not getting too far forward so that a slight peck would send you head-first over his ears, nor being too far back so that if he took off in a gallop you would be left behind. You can decide whether you prefer to sit up against the horse or stay a little forward, both of which work equally well as long as you maintain a safe position in the saddle and do not allow your legs to swing around too much.

Sheer momentum will often decide at what speed you descend slopes and hills but the rider must feel capable of stopping if and when they want. It is a good idea to practise how much control you have by giving yourself stopping points on your way downhill. This will teach your horse to be more responsive as well as helping you to learn how much (if any!) control you have over your mount in such situations. Obviously, if you are coming down a really steep slope, your horse is unlikely to be able to stop immediately and to do so may well put you in a somewhat precarious position, so choose a point that is safe and will not be awkward for the horse.

It is usually best to descend very steep slopes diagonally,

Whether adopting the forward or backward seat going downhill, remember to maintain balance, keep an even feel on the reins and keep the horse going straight.

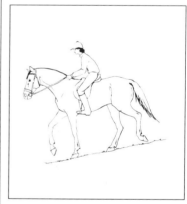

Leaning forward going downhill

Leaning back going downhill

91

zig-zagging across until you reach the bottom. The horse should be allowed to pick his way down on a fairly loose rein, while the rider stays upright in the saddle and pushes their lower leg forwards as a brace. Less steep slopes can usually be trotted or cantered down, either on a looser rein or well supported by the rider. Some horses will do it all on their own; some will require help in balancing and also encouragement to help them down.

If your horse finds it difficult, or you feel insecure, riding up and down hills, then you will need to practise as much as possible. Keep the coming down slow to start with and avoid very steep hills. Inevitably, hills put a strain on legs and tendons, so too much is not a good thing, especially if the horse is not fully fit, but it is very important that you should feel secure and confident about how to ride up and down them before tackling fences on such terrain.

Pulling up

One of the most important points to remember when riding is that you must be under control at all times. All too often, riders can be seen disappearing into the distance, totally out of control! Not only is this dangerous to horse, rider and any poor unfortunate person in the way, it is also extremely frightening.

The reason that horses get out of control is usually that the rider sets off with too long a rein. The free-going horse inevitably soon starts to go faster and the rider finds himself in the position of being unable to shorten the rein any more without letting go to take another grip – not a very comforting thought when you are already out of control.

Always shorten your reins when you start to increase speed, whether intending to gallop or not. If you are going to gallop and jump seriously, you should, anyway, have shortened your stirrups, which gives you more leverage to be able to sit up against your horse. To get a proper reaction from the horse, your hand should be asking through a softening, then shortening, softening, then shortening, action on the rein. With a well-schooled horse, this should coincide with pressure from the legs and seat to rebalance your horse from a forward position, bringing his hocks more underneath him to bring him back to a slower pace.

Unfortunately, with the less well-schooled horse, such use of the legs has the effect of making him go faster as he is probably only used to the legs as a 'go' aid. Hopefully, he may also

These two horses look fairly controlled but the nearside one could easily get out of control if the rider does not take a slightly shorter and then softer hold on the rein. Both horses are wearing standing martingales to stop their heads coming too high.

understand that the pull on the reins means 'stop'. If he does not respond to this when asked, there are various options to which you can resort! For all of them you must remain calm, as nothing makes a horse go faster than a panicking rider. It may be some comfort to know that, generally, the horse does not want to hurt himself any more than you do!

Start by taking a shorter and firmer grip on the reins and being quite positive with your stop aids; sit up well and be very firm. If this produces little response, take a quick look about and start to pull your horse round in a circle, gradually making this smaller and smaller in whichever direction he is

93

most responsive. Keep up a firm pull with the inside rein, while also using your outside rein to keep him balanced.

Try to stay forward so that you can keep a short rein and have a better chance of getting a good grip on the reins. If there is a large hedge that is definitely too high to jump, you can aim towards that, so that at least you will be sure he will slow or turn as he comes towards it. Grab the opportunity of the turn to keep him coming round, as a horse has to slow up when turning, but grip tightly as he decides which way to go!

If there are hills, make use of the up ones – again, he will have to go slower uphill, so find the steepest part and head up there – yell at people in front to warn them of your approach. Once you feel slow enough to turn, pull round in a small circle.

If you are lucky enough to find yourself near some plough, get on to it quickly as this will soon slow up your horse. Again, use the circling method if possible and, once you have managed to stop, try to relax both yourself and the horse, who may well have been as frightened as you by the experience. Do not, whatever you may feel, take it out on the horse – you allowed yourself to get into the situation and, by overreacting now, can only make it worse for the future.

This is definitely the time to reassess your brakes. However, never forget that the horse usually runs away for a reason, which can be anything from fear, fright, over-exuberance to pain as well as inadequate brakes. You may well have contributed to the cause, however unwittingly, so try to work out what caused this reaction from the horse. Were you too slow in realizing what was in his mind; was he frightened by something; were you being too rough with your hands so that he stuck his head up to avoid the pain, was he feeling too fresh and perhaps being overfed – numerous reasons could have caused such behaviour but, whatever happens, you certainly do not want it to happen again. Once both you and he have settled down, for both your sakes it is a good idea to go off quietly and just practise stopping and starting in walk and trot to restore confidence.

Extra exercises for fitness

Apart from the more energetic forms of exercise mentioned earlier, there are a few special exercises that can help with strong horses and generally aid your riding fitness, which you can practise in the comfort of your own home. Press-ups are very useful if you have a strong-pulling horse. Start with two or three if you have never done them before and slowly work up to ten to fifteen if you can. This is much more strenuous than it sounds but it will certainly help your shoulders and biceps. I found it the only way to ensure that I could hold one particularly strong horse.

Lie flat on the floor, face down, and place your hands, palms down, just under your chest. Push up by pressing down onto your hands as you raise your chest and body up. Keep your body taut as you come up, so that the whole body is lifted flat.

Another exercise that is quite useful for strengthening the arms is to stand a couple of feet away from a closed door or wall and push yourself away from this 20 to 30 times. For those who cannot do the former exercise, this is the one to start with.

If you are stiff in your back, gradually bending down to touch your toes is excellent. Start by standing upright, then fold yourself down from the waist and let your body flop downwards. Say to yourself 'Down, one, two, three', trying to get nearer the floor each time before returning to the upright position. Repeat three times to start with and then, as you practise more often, increase the number of times you do this until you find it easy. Anyone who has a back problem should discuss with their doctor or 'back person' what type of exercise should be avoided in case they aggravate an old injury. A pulling horse is never a good thing for a problem back.

Lying flat on your stomach, with your arms folded under your face while lifting the legs, is another useful exercise. It is best to place a cushion or pillow under your pelvis when doing this exercise. Lift the legs by swinging them up three times, then relax before repeating. Start gradually and then do a few more each time, up to a maximum of ten to fifteen.

If you find it difficult to really relax and stretch down with your legs on the horse, you may need to do a few stretching exercises. Stand with your legs about 46 cm (18 in) apart and bend your knees, rising up and down as you would when trotting. Gradually get down lower and lower. This will also help to strengthen your knees. Try to stay erect when doing this, so that you do not get into the habit of tipping forward.

Some people find it difficult to relax their ankle joints. Standing up on tip-toe and sinking down on to your heels will certainly help. Once you have done this, try balancing on the edge of a step of the stairs, holding on to the bannister, and allow your heels to sink down. With practice, your ankles will gradually start to give a little.

The hip, knee and ankle joints are the ones that have to work hard when riding, so any form of bending and stretching is helpful, particularly that of sinking down into a squat position and rising up again, by pushing up rather than pulling yourself up by your hands on the edge of something. This sort of exercise can easily be done in a kitchen. When taking things out of cupboards etc., always sink down to open your cupboards as you would for the exercise and then push yourself up again.

All these exercises, along with general training, will help to prepare you and your horse for competitive work. The following chapter explains how to set about coping with the jumping side of things, in preparation for having a serious go at hunter trials. There is nothing better than being able to tackle courses confidently as they come along, knowing that you have prepared yourself and your horse in the best way.

CHAPTER 3

JUMPING CROSS COUNTRY FENCES

Although you and your horse may well be capable of galloping round a course of cross country fences without too many worries, it is always helpful to know as much as possible about the whys and wherefores, dos and don'ts that can turn your day into a disaster should things ever go wrong. You may have a horse that knows it all anyway, so that you just sit on top and steer. This is a wonderful feeling and the ideal way to build up confidence to jump all sorts of different fences.

This horse is rounding his back well over this cross country fence but the rider is looking down instead of ahead.

The height will depend on your horse's ability and how brave you both feel.

There comes a time, however, when you need to know a little more about what you are doing if you want to progress or bring on a young or less-experienced horse. Many fences require jumping in different ways if they are to be negotiated safely. You do not want to be one of the many Kamikaze riders who fly round on a wing and a prayer, sometimes making it and sometimes not. These people rarely get away with things for long and usually end up with a big problem. It may be a horse that will not go because it has been badly ridden for so long that it has had enough, or a horse that gives them a crashing fall because it simply has not had the schooling to be able to cope with its rider as well as the fences, or they themselves lose confidence and give up.

All of the above are common and it is very sad as, with a little help and greater understanding, many could have a wonderful time if they persevered and set about learning a bit more about what is involved in their chosen sport. I have been riding and competing for over 40 years and still find it amazing how much there is to learn. I am still picking up ideas and learning from mistakes almost daily!

The rest of this chapter is really all about jumping fences of different sorts and coping with the different conditions likely to be met when competing.

Ground conditions

The ground you ride over can have quite an affect on your horse's way of going and it will certainly help if you know how he will react to hard and slippery ground, wet and slippery ground or really deep going. For some horses it seems to make little difference, for others it can be a real handicap.

As far as jumping is concerned, the hard ground can be very jarring, so most horses will not jump extravagantly over fences on hard ground for very long. Older horses, in particular, may begin to shorten their stride and will soon tend to put in short strides before their fences in an effort to reduce the effect of a big jump. They will also tend to avoid jumping boldly over a fence and start just to skim over the top. Some may even begin to stop if it all involves too much of an effort.

For young horses, who need to be given confidence early on and need to enjoy what they are doing from the start, the best way of putting them off is to ask them to jump endlessly on hard ground. Often, the jarring effect on their legs will lead to the development of splints (bony growths on the cannon bones), which are painful when forming and can cause lameness, as well as windgalls (soft swellings around the fetlock joints).

To avoid these problems, try not to ask too much of your horse when the ground is hard and arrange your programme so that you are likely to do more strenuous work in the spring and autumn when it should be softer. Occasional work on hard ground does not usually worry the horse as long as it is not overdone, but daily hammering certainly does.

Hard ground can also be very slippery. If you are competing, remember to be careful when turning or cornering as it is very easy to slip over, which could be extremely painful. It is worth considering small studs for such conditions. If you think these might help, ask your farrier to put in stud holes so that you can use these whenever you need them.

Slippery soft ground can cause other problems. The horse can quickly lose confidence through slithering all over the place on turns and approaches to fences so it is important that you keep him balanced on such ground and canter in an even rhythm. Large studs will certainly help to give a bit of grip and are probably at their most effective on this type of ground. Some people put them in just behind the others, all round.

When riding in slippery conditions, you will need to keep your horse well supported and avoid sharp turns. It is important to come in straight at all your fences in these conditions as slips are particularly liable to occur if you approach off a turn. Avoid excessive acceleration into your fences and abrupt turns before or after them if you can. Pull up gradually, as this is a classic time for slips and slithers.

Really deep ground is much less slippery but has the effect of 'holding' the horse, which restricts his normal forward movement. The deepness of the ground also makes the fences correspondingly bigger, which is something that can make an enormous difference to your horse. The fences may be only 79 cm (3 ft 3 in), according to the measuring stick but for the poor horse jumping out of 7 cm (3 in) of mud, they will be all of 106 cm (3 ft 6 in) which can make a big difference, especially as every stride costs twice the effort it would do in good going.

Studs usually have little effect in this type of going and it is worth remembering that, however fit your horse, he is going to be working a lot harder than usual when tackling fences over this type of ground. By the end of the course he is going to be quite tired and will need all the help he can get from his rider.

Deep going tends to be at its worst at the bottom of hills or where it is particularly wet. Sometimes you may find the going very inconsistent, with the ground soft and deep in some places and relatively firm in others. This type of ground is the most likely to cause problems as both you and the horse can get used to a certain depth of ground and adjust to it. However, when it alters frequently, it is difficult to stay in balance or for the horse to cope easily and injuries are common on such ground. Overreaches, strains to tendons and occasionally to backs and shoulders can result, so try to let the horse find his own balance and speed in such conditions or, if possible, save him for another day.

Assessing the fences

When looking at the fences you are going to jump, you need to take in the type of fence it is – upright, spread, combination, drop or jump up, etc. – and what the approach is like as well as the landing on the other side.

Below and opposite: **This rider has made a well-judged jump over an upright rail. She has supported the horse on take-off, given nicely with her hands over the fence and is starting to sit up for the landing, helping the horse to remain nicely balanced.**

Opposite and above: This is another example of a good jump over a different type of upright – Helsinki steps on the side of a hill. The horse is making a particularly nice 'bascule' over the top of the fence, with the rider staying in balance but giving the necessary freedom with the hands.

Uprights

For upright fences on flat ground, you can usually keep up an even rhythm and support the horse on the approach, making sure he is going forward well, but not too fast, with his eye on the fence. Keep in balance and always try to approach each fence straight, to make it as easy as possible.

If there is an upright, single fence going uphill, you must be aware of the extra effort required for the horse to be able to clear it easily. Galloping uphill too fast will only tire the horse so that, by the time he gets to the fence, he may well have run out of the necessary energy required to negotiate it. Conserve his energy by containing this between your hand and leg in a steady rhythm and pace and, as you approach the fence, really use your legs to push his hind legs more underneath him and enable him to make a good jump.

For an upright fence going downhill, you must ensure that you have sufficient control and ask your horse to remain steady and balanced without getting too much on his forehand. His weight must be back on his hind legs, enabling the front end to spring off the ground easily without its own weight, and that of the jockey, so far forward to be a hindrance.

103

If the horse goes downhill too fast, he will inevitably get out of balance and on to his forehand and it will then be impossible for him to jump out over such a fence safely. Relying on luck is not the answer – your horse must be listening to you. You must sit up and keep him under control at such fences, which are then no problem and great fun to ride.

Generally, you do not want to get too close to an upright fence but should judge your take-off point to be the equivalent of at least the height of the fence in distance in front of the fence when riding slowly and more when travelling faster. If you get too close, you will be liable to hit it on the way up with the front legs. If too far away, it may be the hind legs that catch, depending on the type of jump the horse makes. In deeper going you must aim to take off at the right distance away for that fence as the horse will need to be very athletic in the mud anyway and will already have enough to cope with. Remember to look at the front of your fence to judge your take-off point.

Spread fences

Spread fences may be solid or constructed rather like two uprights, one behind the other. They may have a lower front rail or be of the same height. The front part of the fence should, however, never be higher than the back as the horse finds it difficult to differentiate two different heights in its perspective of the fence and this could result in a nasty fall.

Generally, spread fences are constructed so that they are not greater in width than their height, although the degrees of width vary considerably depending on their design. Some are wider at the bottom than the top, some are square, requiring an accurate jump, others rounded, requiring less accuracy. The wider the fence, the more impulsion is required to clear it, although this obviously depends on the size of the fence in relation to the size of the horse and also its ability.

Spread fences are tremendous fun to jump and, because of their rather more imposing appearance, are usually respected and cleared well by the horse, providing he is ridden forward well and in balance on the approach. There is nothing more demoralizing for the horse than being ridden too slowly at a spread fence, which then requires a tremendous effort to clear it. Approaching too slowly may well result in the back legs hitting the fence and, if this happens too often, the horse will soon decide that such fences are no fun at all.

Ride the horse forward into a good, balanced contact and keep your leg on throughout so that his controlled impulsion

Tyres are an excellent introduction to a spread fence which requires a little more effort from the horse. Both horse and rider look very happy but the rider's knee has come away from the saddle which does not add to security!

This is a wider spread over a sheep feeder which has the added problem of a roof. Practise over as many fences of different designs as you can, so that the horse is confident about all types.

is released forward over the fence. Your actual speed will depend on all sorts of factors such as where you are on the course, whether it is up- or downhill, the going, etc., but the horse must always be going forward in front of your leg and have the freedom to stretch out over these fences. 'If in doubt, kick on' is an excellent bit of advice for all fences and especially for a spread. Spread fences should never be met on a decreasing stride, when the horse will be losing his forward impulsion.

For the spread fence that has an uphill approach, remember to really drive your horse forward in the last few strides as the uphill effort will have resulted in a less forward stride. Keep him going on landing so that you make it easy for him afterwards as well.

Unlike the upright, you need to adjust your take-off point for the spread fence to be closer to the base, as the highest point of the horse's jump will be over the centre of the fence in most cases. If you ask him to take off too far away, you are risking the danger of not being able to clear the width with ease – you may get away with it over small fences but, as they get bigger, you will quickly start to undermine the horse's confidence if he has to overstretch too often.

Some spread fences have the highest part of the spread at the back of the fence, as in a triple bar or some zig-zag fences. These fences are designed to encourage the horse to jump out in a wider jumping arc, and your take-off point needs to be very close to the base of the fence so that the highest point of the jump is over the highest part of the fence. A horse moving at speed will jump out a surprisingly long way if he has met the fence on a good stride and his rider is going with him and in balance.

For spread fences coming downhill, the secret is to stay balanced and keep the horse under control. They will have impulsion anyway in most cases but do need supporting so that they can get their hocks under them to clear the fence cleanly in front. When coming down a hill the horse's balance will, inevitably, tend to be forwards, so you must ensure that he can lift his forehand by sitting up and keeping hold of his head until he is airborne and then be ready to keep him controlled on landing.

If, for any reason, he begins to slow up coming downhill, you must sit up and drive him forward with your legs. Some horses are naturally cautious down hills but nearly all will require some balancing, with the hand as support, and then positive riding over the actual fence.

107

The most usual spread fences to be found on cross country courses are things like log pile, parallels, sleeper tables and hedges. Trakehners with ditches underneath and tiger traps or elephant traps all sound rather horrifying but simply require positive riding forwards, just like every other spread fence.

Fences with ditches before, underneath or afterwards are fairly classic 'rider frighteners' and must be ridden at positively. Never look down into a ditch but forward and over it. Psychologically, looking down into anything means a loss of forward movement and the horse will tend to sense your reaction, wonder what the problem is and also slow down, losing that vital impulsion that is so necessary to make the fence easy to jump. Inevitably, if this happens too often, he will also start to wonder about such fences and then you have both horse and rider with a self-made 'hang up' about a certain type of fence. Be positive, look forward and, for goodness sake, do not let your nerves take over – it is such a wonderful feeling to get round a course clear that a few hard kicks will be well worth the effort!

Simple combinations

Most hunter trials will have some sort of combination somewhere on the course. These may be very straightforward in the small events and on Novice courses but all require a little thought to get them right and ensure you negotiate them with ease.

The first rule is to keep straight, as these fences are likely to consist of a simple in-and-out in their basic form, with varying numbers of strides in between each obstacle. Two fences of the sort usually known as either a double, as in show jumping, or as single combination, in-and-out, or whatever, are normally judged as one fence.

The fence will be numbered as, say, '10', with the first part being '10A' and the second part, '10B'. Because it is basically one fence, should you have problems, you will be eliminated if you have more than two refusals at either part, which must be negotiated in the correct sequence. However, the good thing is that if you jump part A successfully and then stop at B, you do not have to go back and do A again – only the last element. (You can do the whole thing again if you want to but if you then stop at A, having already jumped it, it will still count as a second refusal.) Some combinations may have more elements, such as a third and, very rarely, a fourth element as C and D. The same principle applies. As long as you have negotiated the fences in sequence, if you have a refusal at one you

This horse is practising jumping a rail, to ditch, to a rail, with one stride between each element. The rider has a good leg position and has given freedom nicely when the horse has stretched over the ditch.

Jumping combinations requires better balance and quick readjustment between the elements of the fence.

do not have to re-jump those already negotiated unless you especially want to or it is easier to do so.

Scoring at combinations

The scoring for such fences is 20 penalties for the first refusal, run out or circle, 40 for the second at the same fence, regardless of whether or not it was at the same part of the fence, and elimination for a third refusal, run out or circle. For a fall, 60 penalties are given. These scores are based on those used in horse trials, which are now used in hunter trials more or less universally, but occasionally there will be a different scale, which will be printed in the schedule or programme.

The diagrams on page 16 show what are regarded as refusals, run outs or circles in between fences or different elements of fences. It is important to understand fully the difference between fences numbered separately but set close

together and those close together but classed as one fence or combination. If you jump a separately numbered fence twice, you will be eliminated, as you have already negotiated that obstacle.

A fast approach can undermine confidence. This hair-raising jump was caused by an unbalanced approach.

Jumping combinations

Most simple combinations can be jumped as you would any upright or spread fence if there are more than two non-jumping strides in between the parts. You must approach them straight, so that your horse is in no doubt that there are two fences here, to be jumped one after the other. If you do not come in straight, it will be very easy for the horse to run out, usually at the second part. Keep your reins a little shorter, so that you can react quickly if a run out is likely to happen, and hold him on a straight line from one fence to the next.

Occasionally, your combination fences will be closer

111

Some fences in team chases include a type of pen into which two or three horses must jump before one is allowed to jump out.

together and you should pace out how many strides your horse is likely to take in between the first and last part and then control him enough to make this easy if just one or two strides are required. If you approach a combination too fast, the horse will jump in too far over the first part to be able to put in the intended number of strides to jump out safely. He might try to bounce out with no stride at all or put in an awkward small stride, which can be very uncomfortable and, in some cases, rather unsafe if he is unable to balance himself for the out part. Some horses panic when they feel unsafe and stop very quickly, depositing their riders straight over their heads. Others simply fail to leave the ground, with equally disastrous results.

Always steady and balance your horse before approaching a combination fence, so that he is sufficiently back on his hocks to be able to jump safely through the obstacle. This

will also give the horse the necessary time to assess what he has to do, enabling him to put in a better jump. Try to sit up a bit on the approach and again on landing over the first part, so that you help the horse to rebalance himself quickly rather than having your extra weight too far forward, making it more difficult to recover from the jump.

Some combinations ask you to jump in over one fence and then turn and come out in another direction. This requires a bit more control and the rider will have to be quick to indicate to the horse where it is supposed to go and then ride positively to ensure this actually happens. Because your horse is probably more used to going straight, he may be a bit reluctant to turn in the middle of the course unless you have practised this sort of thing.

You may come across a 'pen fence' at hunter trials, which sometimes requires you to jump in and do something specific before jumping out again. In pairs or team chases, they generally want you to jump in with two or three horses before allowing you to jump out. With rather keen and excitable horses in the middle of a cross country round, this can be easier said than done. Keep your horse turning quietly until you are set to go again if he is getting overkeen.

Sometimes a Normandy bank combination is included, which involves jumping up on to a bank as part A and then down off the bank over a rail or log as part B, with a bit of a drop landing. Keep riding forwards and give your reins well over the drop.

Banks

Banks are especially common in certain parts of the UK, and in Ireland where they are a common sight in the countryside. However, man-made banks are very expensive to build, so comparatively few are likely to be found in hunter trials. If they are narrow, the horse will probably fly them without putting a foot down unless they are very high, so they need riding on at to encourage the horse to do this. Sit fairly upright so that you are prepared in case he puts a foot down on the bank.

Below and opposite: **Jumping on and off banks needs practice by both the rider and the horse. You need to stay forward well on the way up and stay in balance on the way down, either sitting up as this rider is doing or going forward – whichever you find easier. Be careful never to get too far forward in front of the movement of the horse.**

Steps

Steps need a certain amount of preparation as you approach them, whether going up or down, but much the same mixture of balance and impulsion is required as for banks. When going up, make sure you are straight and have the horse going well forward. You must not let him come to the fence on a long rein but must have his energy bottled up, ready for the effort required to continue to jump upwards over the two, three or however many steps are to be negotiated. If you are not straight, the steps will be wider for the horse and therefore will become more strenuous.

The more steps there are, the more effort is required and you must also be aware that, with each jump upwards, the horse is likely to land a bit shorter, so remember to help him by continuing to drive him forwards right to the top; do not just give up once he has taken off at the first step. Keep your weight forward and your seat out of the saddle so that you are helping as much as possible. If you lose balance and get left behind, keep kicking him on and grab some mane or hang on to the neckstrap or your martingale, so that you do not

Below and opposite: **This sequence shows the rider dropping down over a couple of steps into water. She is in a good, safe position but her legs are firmly urging the horse forward. She has given the rein enough to allow the horse to stretch forward, yet has still kept him straight.**

catch him in the mouth, which would badly interfere with his forward effort.

Sometimes there is a step up, followed, a stride or two later, by a post and rails. The same sort of effort is required to negotiate this – keep the horse going forward and keep riding until you are over the rail; keep your weight forward.

For steps going down, the first point to remember is that, in most cases, the horse will not be able to see anything on the approach as these fences are built into a downhill slope, so slow up as you come towards the fence and sit up and push him up together to get his hocks underneath him ready for the jump down. If you come towards steps too fast and the horse only realizes at the last minute that there is a jump down, he is likely to do one of two things. Either he will continue on and jump down too fast, with the danger of landing on the edge of one step or even missing it altogether, creating the possibility of falling; or the more cautious horse is likely to stop dead at the top to assess the situation. There is every likelihood that you will not stay with him and will land with a painful bump after hurtling over his ears onto the lower step!

A fast approach can undermine the horse's confidence as, in either of the above situations, the horse will have been presented with a shock jump, caused entirely by the way the rider brought him into it. Always try to imagine how your horse will see something and remember what your own thoughts

When jumping steps choose the most direct line up through them and then keep as straight as possible, riding strongly upwards.

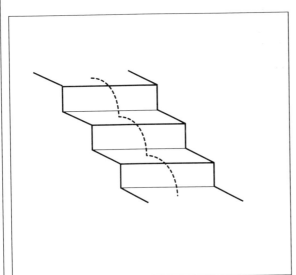

By going straight up the middle the step width can easily be judged

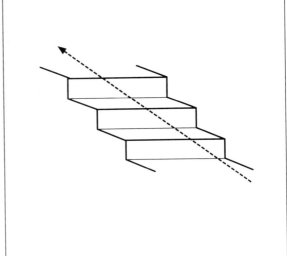

By angling the steps you are asking the horse to make a greater effort as the angle and depth will be increased

were when walking the course – if they were something like 'Oh help, what on earth have we got now' as you approached on foot, the horse's thoughts might well be the same. You have the advantage of knowing what is coming and that, in fact, it is all perfectly possible – he does not.

Steps down need a steady approach and are generally best jumped from a controlled canter or a forward-going trot. Sit up well on the approach, keep your leg on to keep the horse going forward and be ready to slip the reins through your fingers to give him the freedom of his head as he jumps down. The cautious horse may be a bit hesitant, so be very positive and, if necessary, use your whip to give him an encouraging, sharp tap behind the girth. A single step back in competition could count as a refusal, so you must be ready to keep him going forward throughout. Ideally, if the horse can learn over small steps, or over one at a time, and get his technique right by lowering himself down economically, he will not jar himself, which tends to happen if he gives too exaggerated a jump or goes too fast. It can be helpful to practise quietly over small steps if the horse is worried about this type of obstacle but, once mastered, steps are fun to ride.

Ditches

Ditches come in a variety of forms but are one of the fences riders tend to get worried about. They normally consist of a dug-out, narrow trench and may be either part of a natural drainage ditch or one made specifically for the fence. They can be wide or narrow, deep or shallow, frightening to look at or very insignificant. They may be a jump on their own or incorporated into a fence.

Basically, a ditch on its own is one of the most simple fences as it requires no height and, if you bear in mind that the average horse's stride is 3.6 m (12 ft) and that you rarely meet a single ditch that is anywhere near that, or even half of that, it only goes to show how simple they are. What really bothers people seems to be the depth, which, quite honestly, is immaterial! The secret with ditches is always to ride on and look forwards over them, never down into them.

From the horse's point of view, they require little effort but some may appear a little spooky, so introduce your horse to little ones to start with. Once he realizes what is required and as long as he has never been frightened by slipping into one and then not given proper schooling immediately afterwards, he is unlikely to find them difficult. Schooling with another horse can be very helpful initially but is rarely necessary if

Some ditches have rails over them which encourages the horse to jump up as well as out. This small trakehner-type is being jumped well.

you start over small and not too deep ditches. Practise jumping backwards and forwards and seize every opportunity you can to jump as many as possible. Make sure the take-off and landing are secure and that there are no holes on either side.

In general, single ditches require positive riding with a strong, forward and balanced stride. Look up and sit up on the approach, keeping your horse going forward and in front of your leg. If the ditch is only a small one, there is little need to increase the stride but for the wider ones you can ride on a little more and encourage the horse to jump up a little more so that it is easier to clear the width.

For fences with ditches before or after them, such as open

ditches (a hedge with a ditch in front), you can really set your horse alight and ride on so that you get a really big bold leap over the fence, which is a lovely feeling, similar to that felt by jockeys in steeplechasing. The same goes for ditches on the landing side. Ride on strongly as the horse cannot see them anyway, so it is important to have enough speed and impulsion to encourage the horse to jump out and clear them with ease. If going too slowly, the horse will make too big an arc over the fence and will land too steeply, so you want to create impulsion that is carried forward with speed.

The classic combination fence incorporating a ditch is the coffin, which consists of rails to a ditch followed by rails, with one or two strides in between each element. This is very often built where there is a slope down to the ditch and requires a balanced, but forward, approach without being too fast. You must sit up so that you do not get in front of the horse but can keep him moving forward well. Coffins built on the flat require a definite steadying of the horse, so that he has the chance to fit in the necessary strides. Too fast and he could be encourage to miss one out, with the possible result of a fall as he ends up either too close or too far away from one of the elements.

Trakehners and tiger traps have already been discussed under spreads. They require positive riding so that the spread is easy. If your horse is a little spooky, he could tend to slow down 'to have a look' and thus lose some of his forward impulsion. Be positive and, if necessary, take your whip hand off the rein and use the whip behind the girth to ensure that he is going at the right pace to make an easy jump.

Occasionally, you will find water ditches or open water ditches, which are usually wider ditches filled with water. There is nothing different about these except to stick to the rule of riding straight and positively. If your horse is used to water, he should have no worries, but sit up and ride him well forwards from the leg so that he makes a good clean jump from one bank to the other.

Corners

Corners do occasionally appear in hunter trial courses, so it is important that you know how to jump them before you meet them in competition. They will have an apex end (the corner) with the ends usually widening out to give the option of a bounce jump or, at the far end, an in-and-out, usually with one stride in between.

The corner requires an accurate, balanced piece of riding

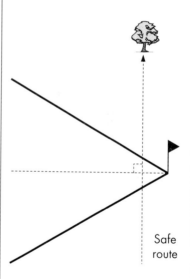

Safe route

It is most important to dissect the angle and jump at right angles to this over corners. Look behind you and then at an obvious landmark ahead to ensure you keep on a good line.

121

Opposite and above: The author is schooling over a corner fence which requires accurate, bold riding over the apex end of the fence. Both horse and rider seem so confident that they finish the jump with their eyes closed!

to ensure that you jump the exact spot you have chosen as safe and best to jump. This should be just in from the apex, before the fence starts to widen out and, in fact, is nothing more than a spread with a very accurate approach. When you walk the course, walk backwards a few strides from the fence, line yourself up to a chosen point beyond the fence and then decide on a point in front of the fence from where you can get on to a definite line. This must lead straight over the jumpable part of the fence. Once you are lined up, make sure you keep your horse going strongly forward and stay on that line.

Water

Water fences often appear in hunter trial courses in some shape or other. They may be in the form of a 'splash' or as a more definite type of fence with a log or rails in or out or both. The most important thing from the horse's point of view is to know that the bottom is safe and firm without holes that could cause him to stumble or fall. The test for the horse is going into the water. He is not going to know whether it is 10 cm or 50 cm deep but he must have enough trust in you to

123

believe that it is safe. Make sure you either walk through the water to check the surface or watch a few others ride through to ensure that it all looks easy and safe.

Speed and water do not go well together as excessive speed creates a lot of spray, making it impossible to see your way through, while deep water will create a lot of drag on the horse's legs, which can unbalance or trip him. A strong, positive approach without excessive speed is best – some people like to canter; some prefer a good forward-going trot. Remember that you are going to have a slight drop going in whatever the design of the fence, so sit up well and do not allow yourself to flop forwards on landing, making it all more difficult. Remember to slip your reins through your fingers if the horse needs it.

If your horse is unsure of water, take every opportunity you can to ride him through big puddles and streams, etc. but always be sure that the bottom is safe and secure. Nothing will undermine a horse's confidence more than to find himself floundering around in deep water with an uneven, boggy base.

The spray created can be lessened if you slow up as soon as you get into the water and then go forward once the horse has been able to see what is required on the way out. This may involve a jump out, in which case ride the horse strongly as the drag of the water can hinder his efforts coming out, making it a bit more difficult than a fence on dry land.

If there is no fence but you have to go through a river or stream, it will probably have a gradual approach into the water but some horses do not like the initial thought of getting their feet wet. Keep urging him forward and encouraging him with soothing words if he is frightened or, if necessary, use your stick behind the girth and be very positive. The water may be quite deep in the middle; do not panic but allow the horse to pick his way through. Concentrate on what he is doing. Occasionally the urge to roll takes hold and if you do not keep moving he may decide to take a dip – always keep moving in water, even when it is deep, so that this does not happen. If the water is very deep and you are on a pony or small horse, draw your legs up like a jockey so that your boots do not fill with water – it will only be for a stride or two unless you have gone very far off-course!

Drops

The drop fence comes many designs and for all of them it is the landing that is really the point of issue. It may present as a drop off a bank, such as a Normandy bank, into water as

Right: The rider has adopted a backward seat over this drop fence, remaining in excellent balance with a secure lower leg and sympathetic hands.

Below: The author, jumping off a bank, is using the forward seat. This is just as effective and secure as the seat shown in the picture above.

By going slowly over a drop fence such as this, you avoid jarring the horse. If you go too fast you will land much further down the slope and there is a greater risk of a peck or fall and of jarring the horse's front legs unnecessarily.

previously discussed, over a hedge with a drop landing, over a downhill fence of any sort or just off a bit of higher ground to lower ground as a single step.

With all drop landings, the important point always to think about is that the weight of the rider must remain in balance at all times so that you do not add to the horse's effort by hindering him unnecessarily. Sit up and brace yourself a bit more than for a jump on the flat. Use your legs to help to keep yourself more upright, by pushing them forward once you have taken off, so that they act as supports whether you adopt a forward or backward seat over the actual obstacle.

It is important to give the horse the freedom he needs over these fences, so the ability to 'slip the reins' is vital. This does not mean letting them go but allowing your fingers to open so that the horse can take as much rein as he needs to stretch down over these fences. You can gather them back again immediately on landing. Keep the contact on the approach, however, so that your jump is controlled.

Your speed of approach is governed by the type of fence involved. A wider fence will need a bit more pace to clear the width than an upright, so you will need to ride on a bit over the former and remain steadier over the upright.

The faster you go over a fence with a drop, the further out you will jump and, in some cases, the more you are likely to jar your horse, so look at the landing carefully and assess which way you need to tackle it. A flat landing is much more jarring to a horse than one that continues on down, however awe-inspiring the latter may appear. A slight drop will make little difference to the horse but as it gets bigger, the state of the ground and the landing itself will have a bigger impression. Hard ground and too many drop fences will soon make your horse shorten his stride and become reluctant to tackle these fences in his usual style.

Ski-jumps

A rather unusual fence that may be encountered is the ski-jump. This generally involves riding up a steep hill or ramp, with or without much of a fence, often a log, at the top and then descending down either a very steep slope or a slide on the other side. In more advanced competitions this may have a fence at the bottom, which will require a controlled descent.

The way to tackle these obstacles is to ride strongly up the slope or ramp and keep urging the horse on until you are over the log or whatever at the top. Stick your legs forwards at the top and allow the horse to lower himself down as he chooses

127

but keep him straight and under control if there is a fence to jump at the bottom. If not, keep the momentum going forwards, stay upright and be ready to slip your reins if necessary.

Heights of fences

The height of the fences will affect the way you ride many of them and your own experience, combined with that of the horse, will determine what size of fences you should be jumping. There are no hard and fast rules as so much of successful jumping is based on mutual confidence between horse and rider. It is, however, a mistake to try to jump fences that are too high for the current ability of either of you. Things may be fine when everything goes right but problems arise when they start to go wrong. An experienced rider is able to help the horse or to realize what has caused the problem and set about putting it right before it gets worse. An inexperienced one is not able to do this and so often the situation can go from bad to worse.

As a rough guide, start small and do not go up to the next height, usually 7.5 cm (3 in) higher, until you feel confident and have successfully negotiated your last three courses without a problem. There are numerous ways of maintaining progress without necessarily going higher. Each time you go out, think of one aspect that you are going to work on – it can be speed, control, approach to the fences, style over them, rhythm throughout, balance up and down hills – there are so many different things to work on.

Control on the course

One of the most important factors is feeling safe and control is vital to this. Very often, it is not until you are actually at the competition that the horse starts to get too strong to hold. There are several reasons why this can happen, any of which might be affecting your particular horse. The most usual is that the horse becomes a little excited so that he does not respond to your wishes as he normally would at home. He may become a bit wild and no longer listen. Very often, all he needs to bring him back to his normal self is twenty minutes on a circle in a quiet corner, twisting and turning to the right and left quite quietly. Once he starts to listen to you in trot, canter him again on the circle in the forward jumping position, with your reins quite short. Keep him going until he really settles down. Control and obedience are vital, so be

This horse and rider look full of confidence and appear ready to tackle bigger fences.

quite sure that he is listening to you and responding before plunging into the midst of things.

Tightening the noseband a hole or two, if it is fairly loose, may help or the curb chain if you have a curb bit. Many horses do get stronger in competition and may require a stronger bit. If you ride in a snaffle, there are several different designs that can make just that little bit of difference, such as the copper roller, a mixture of copper and steel rollers in the mouthpiece, which, in theory prevents the horse from taking too strong a hold as the rollers swivel. The Magenis bit has rollers within the mouthpiece and the plain roller snaffle is also

This rider is endeavouring to steady her horse with too strong a hand and she is bringing the head up too high in front of the fence which will interfere with the horse's jump. Her main problem, however, is that she is riding too long for cross country.

good: both are designed to prevent the horse taking too strong a hold.

The double-jointed Doctor Bristol, which has a central plate within the joints, works well on some horses. If a curb bit is felt necessary try the Kimblewick or the Pelham. The former can be made with slots for the reins in the D of the cheeks, which accentuates its action. The Pelham can have two reins, the lower curb being used only to achieve greater control, while riding mostly on the top one. Alternatively, roundings can be used. Many people favour these for cross country riding as it involves only one rein but you then lose the effect of the curb as a means of control in itself.

Never forget that many horses are particularly sensitive in their mouths and this is accentuated at an outing. It may well be that, in the excitement of the occasion, you are tightening

your hands and restricting your horse more than he can bear in the circumstances and all that he needs is a softer, more sympathetic hand and a bit of confidence. There is a very true saying that 'It's the hands at the end of the reins, not the bit, that control the horse'.

Do not forget the importance of a martingale for control. A correctly fitted running martingale can be extremely effective, especially in turning. For the horse that opens his mouth a lot, a drop or flash noseband can be helpful.

Remember to start off with your reins tight enough in the first place but with that essential relaxed and supple wrist and hand. If your reins are slippery, make sure you are wearing non-slip gloves and have the non-slip type of reins. Check that your stirrups are short enough to prevent you from being pulled forwards with a floppy lower leg.

This rider is maintaining a contact but allowing the horse to sustain his rhythm into the fence, even though her hands are rather straight and high.

131

Slipping the reins

One of the essentials for the cross country rider to master is being able to slip the reins correctly. This allows the horse to have as much freedom over the fence as he needs, according to the circumstances of the jump. Over most fences on the flat it is rarely necessary as the horse should not have to stretch unduly to clear the fence unless he takes off too far away and has to stretch.

Slipping the reins means allowing the reins to be taken by the horse as he needs them to make a successful jump. The rider must open the fingers to free the reins just enough to let them run through the hand. As soon as enough has been taken to negotiate the jump, the hand closes and one hand is taken off the rein to take up the slack again to get ready for the next jump.

This is a particularly important lesson to learn early on in cross country riding as otherwise you will be unable, in some situations, to give the horse the necessary freedom, with the result that he will be caught in the mouth just at the time he requires to stretch his head and neck to the maximum. If this happens too often, he will lose confidence and not want to stretch fully over fences or drops. You can allow your hands and arms to go forward so far but there are always occasions when this is not enough, so you must know how to help the horse when he is at his most vulnerable.

If you find this difficult to do, it can help you to get the feel if you ride with your hand 'down the rein' a few times. This involves holding the rein with your hand underneath and the rein coming through the hand by the thumb and first finger then out over the little finger. This is also helpful if you tend to move your hands too much in front of the fence.

Riding a line

Once you have mastered the art of riding successfully over a course, there are a few more subtleties to be perfected and one of these is that of riding a line through a combination and also from one fence to another on the most economical route.

Although it is unlikely that you will meet a combination that requires too accurate an approach in a hunter trial, there are always a few exceptions, especially those that are very professionally organized or are run over horse trial fences.

The great importance of getting your line right cannot be

Above: **This rider has been left behind at take-off at this fence but has managed to 'slip her reins' to give the horse the necessary freedom over the fence.**

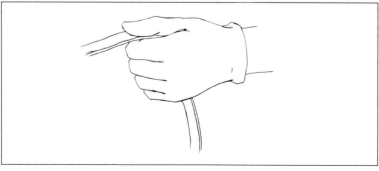

Right: Holding the hand down the rein makes it easier to let your hand go forward with the movement of the horse. This exercise can be very useful if you tend to catch your horse in the mouth a little.

133

overemphasized; it can amount to the difference between an easy ride through a fence and an almost lethal one, when you are asking a horse to take a route where certain stridings affect the degree of difficulty. This has already been discussed briefly in riding corners, where a line through, from before the fence to afterwards, is vital.

You must always look back to where you have come from to ensure that you have not strayed from your best chosen route but have come to the exact spot where you want to start negotiating your combination fence. Whatever form this takes, you must decide on your course walk where it is you want to go and then make sure that this is exactly what you do. It is no good deciding that you want to jump on the right-hand side of a fence to avoid landing on a bad bit of ground and to get an easier view of the next fence if you then approach it on the left. You must be sure where you want to go and then be

The rider has carefully lined up her horse to jump two angled logs and is concentrating on the second part.

Although she has flopped forward over this second fence, the rider has jumped the middle of both elements and has maintained a firm leg position.

very certain that that is where you actually ride on the course. Accuracy counts for more and more as the courses get bigger and you attempt more advanced competitions.

You can save a lot of time over your course by the way you ride from one fence to another. This can be achieved by consciously thinking of your next fence immediately you have jumped the previous one. In this way, you will get on line to the next fence by taking the shortest route. Wide sweeps after one fence before leading to another involve several strides out of your direct line. Even if you only waste a second per fence, that is likely to make you between 16 and 20 seconds slower than a rider who is consciously thinking and looking for the next obstacle and getting there sooner.

When walking the course, always glance back when you are halfway between one fence and another to see if you are on a good line. If can be really surprising how far out you can be,

135

especially on your first walk when you are not too sure where you are going anyway, unless it is one of those courses where you can see all the fences as you walk.

If you have to turn after jumping a fence, do not forget the essential basic of inside hand, outside leg to ensure that your horse responds as quickly as possible. Once you become really experienced, you can start to angle some of the fences on the flat on good ground, saving a second or two on each occasion, but only do this when you are really confident and effective going straight. Remember the importance of being straight over bigger spreads as angling these will make them wider. There is also the danger of the horse dropping a leg down on one of these as he will be unable to bring both legs clear of the fence if angled too acutely and so could be in danger of a fall. Safety should always take priority over speed.

Be a good competitor

In the excitement of going to a competition, make sure you are a popular competitor and be thoughtful to others. Do not hog the practice fence by overusing it and thus preventing others from having a jump. Two or three jumps should be ample to warm your horse up.

If you are having a problem anywhere on the course, always make way for a following competitor before trying again at the fence. If out of control or circling for any reason make sure you are not in anyone else's way and, if so, make sure they are aware of this by yelling (politely), if necessary, to let them know that you are approaching.

In the box park, make sure you do not block anyone in when you park. Some boxes have side as well as back ramps, so ensure that you do not hinder someone else's unboxing arrangements. If you borrow anything, always return it as soon as you have finished with it. Nothing is more annoying than lending something and then having to wait around to find the person before you can leave.

Should you find anything left around, hand it in to the secretary who can have something read out over the public address system or will keep it for a time in case anyone rings up about it.

Be as helpful and polite as you can to everyone, whether it is a good or a bad day, as competitions rely on the goodwill of numerous voluntary helpers who enjoy coming as long as they also have a good day.

CHAPTER 4

COMPETITIONS

If you are a really competitive type of person, no amount of schooling or preparation will equal the big moment of actually riding in a competition itself. It is this that really gets one's blood up, sets the adrenaline flowing and leaves one with a feeling of anticipation that is experienced at no other time. This is the moment you have waited for, to prove to yourself, and maybe others too, that you have got what it takes to set off round a course of strange fences, persuade your horse to respond to your will and negotiate the course to the best of your ability. The feeling of exhilaration on completing is a unique experience and to finish with a clear round is even better.

Entering

The first step towards competing is to choose a competition to enter, that is reasonably nearby, and then acquire a schedule. These can usually be picked up at similar events, local shops, saddlers or riding schools or can be sent for from addresses advertised in the local equestrian press or through riding clubs or the Pony Club.

Look through the classes carefully and check their conditions of entry and regulations. Choose the one most suitable for your standard, based either on heights of fences or experience. The schedule will normally have an entry form attached to it, and will give the close of entries date, which is generally a week to three weeks before the competition. Some events are particularly popular and entries are accepted on a first-come, first-served basis, others accept everyone, regardless of numbers. Enter early to be sure of acceptance. At some competitions you can enter on the day for certain classes, but not all.

Make sure that you have read all the rules for your class

carefully and are eligible, have sent off the correct entry money and have filled in the entry form legibly and correctly. Enclose a stamped, addressed envelope if requested and carefully note if you are to be given starting times. If so, make a note to remind yourself to telephone at the correct time. It is quite maddening for organizers to have people telephoning at all hours of the day and night and they may not have anyone near the telephone anyway if you ring too late. You are usually asked to ring one or two days before the competition.

Preparations

Do not leave everything to the last minute and think ahead if there is anything to purchase before the competition. Check that your horse's shoes are secure. If they are looking a little loose at the beginning of the week, you can more or less guarantee that they will be half-off by the day of your event, so book your farrier if you have any doubts. If you are going to use studs for competing, make sure you have stud holes, that these are cleaned out and that your studs and kit are clean and oiled ready to use.

Check through all your tack and make sure it is clean and ready the day before. Remember that you will need rugs or sheets, a sweat rug, bandages or boots, overreach boots, grooming kit, water, hay and your own clothes including boots, back protector and skull hat.

Do not forget to check the trailer or horsebox if you are using your own transport. Tyres, water, oil and fuel need checking before every journey. Work out your route and have a map with you as well as the schedule and any passes you may have been sent. The schedule normally give good directions to the actual site. Usually there are also signs, although these are occasionally poorly displayed and difficult to spot, let alone understand, so be alert as you near your destination!

Your horse may need a trim up and a mane and tail wash, particularly if he has been out. Try not to subject him to a complete bath the day before as he could easily catch a chill unless it is really hot, which is unlikely at hunter-trial times of the year. It is not necessary to plait for hunter trials but your horse should look neat, with a tidy mane and tail. If you can keep him in the night before the competition, this saves time the next day as otherwise he is bound to find the dirtiest spot in his paddock to roll in and will have wrecked most of your efforts of the day before!

Make sure your horse is clean and tidy before going to the show. If the weather is hot a good bath might be refreshing.

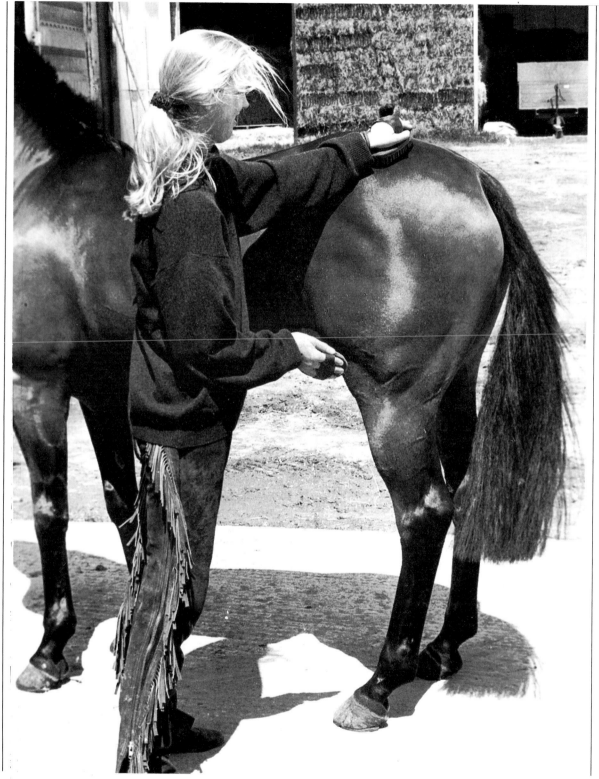

On arrival

Try to park on as flat a bit of ground as possible; if your horse is tilted uncomfortably for too long, he will not think too much of you. This is not always easy, however, if it is a hilly venue or the stewards want the boxes parked in a certain way. If this is the case, let your horse come out of the box and tie him up if he is quiet or take him out and lead him around if he has got a really long wait. He should be all right if it is not more than a couple of hours.

Find out where the secretary's tent is, if things are running on time and whether you need to put your number down or if you are going in numerical order. This is usually covered in the programme, so it is well worth getting one of these on arrival as they also have a list of the fences, which is usually

Keep an eye on your horse in the horsebox park especially in warm weather when he may need an extra drink or lead-out if it is hot inside the box or trailer. Take care that horses are not so close that they could kick one another.

very helpful when you set off to walk the course. Check your times and find out how long before starting you should be in the collecting ring. If this is optional, work out how long it will take from the horsebox park to the collecting ring and practice fence. You do not want to end up being late just because you have not allowed enough time.

Walking the course

If you live not too far away, it may be a good idea to go and walk the course the day before but check that it will be open to do so before setting off. Otherwise, allow plenty of time to do this on the day. An hour should cover most hunter trial courses but some take longer. Two hours minimum should be allowed from your arrival time to the time you are due to

141

start on your course. Allow a longer time if you have not done many competitions or do not know what sort of venue to expect.

Make sure you set off in comfortable footwear as there is nothing worse than discovering at the far side of the course that you have foot blisters! Wellington boots may be necessary if there is a river to cross or a water jump to walk through and it is always worth a taking a pair to an event just in case.

Set off round the course, taking a careful look at all your take-offs and landings. If some of these look a bit sticky early in the day, they are only going to get worse, so you will need to be ready to jump a little more to the right or left of centre where the ground will be at its worse.

Count the fences as you go to make sure you do not miss one out. If there are different courses or classes in the event, be sure you follow the right numbers for yours. Different courses sometimes have different-coloured markers. Watch out for any turning flags. You may have to go through these on the course. They will normally be red and white and you must pass between them, keeping the red one on your right and

Study each fence carefully as you walk your course and know which numbers or colours to follow for your class. This fence, for example, has an L (for 'Learner') and may have a higher fence beside it for other classes. Check your rules to find out if this is relevant to your course.

the white on your left. If there is only one turning flag, the same principle applies. If it is red, keep it on your right; if white keep it on your left.

If possible, walk your course twice so that you are quite familiar with it and will then be able to concentrate on riding each fence rather than worrying whether you ought to turn right or left over the next one. Try to choose a line that will bring you in straight at each fence, to give your horse the best possible chance of jumping it well. Always look at each fence carefully as you approach it and check your reaction, so that you are ready should the horse feel the same later on.

Sometimes, as you come towards a fence into a wood, it can look initially as if there is nowhere safe to go and that it is all a wall of trees. However, if you approach a little more to the right or left, then it becomes apparent that a nice track exists through the trees. Always aim to give your horse confidence by making things easy for him. He will then jump confidently which will, in turn, help you.

Other fences that are rather awe-inspiring on the approach are fences on the brows of hills. They can look very daunting stuck up on the skyline and quite scary at times, so be ready to be really positive so that your horse does not lose heart and give up – when he gets there he will soon see that it is all right but if you do not ride strongly and he is a little uncertain, he will have lost the impulsion to clear it anyway.

Drops downwards over a log always appear spectacular on the approach and here you need to walk along the edge of the fence to see where there is less of a drop and if you can see an easier spot to jump over that looks better on the approach. If the horse is confronted by a bush or something similar as he approaches, he will start to suspect a hazard and not really keep up the forward momentum, so give such fences a good look, equate your initial feelings on first sight of them to those of your horse and act accordingly – usually by controlled but forward riding.

If you can visualize yourself riding each fence as you walk the course, it will help you to appreciate what needs to be done on your approach to each. Some people jot down a few notes beside the drawing or name of each fence in the programme.

If you have the opportunity of watching a few other competitors go round the course as you walk, watch how they go and be really critical so that you can say to yourself, 'I must do that or must not' as the case may be. Watch how they approach the fences and their speed in particular and see

Badminton winner Mary Thompson is in a safe position with this young horse, dropping downhill over a big log.

whether they help their horses or are a hindrance. You will soon spot the ones who know what they are doing and those who do not.

Once you have walked your course, mentally go through it all again, making sure you know exactly where you are going and which places require special attention and then be absolutely certain that you are clear in your mind about your start and, particularly, finishing flags. So often people walk the course and do not pay proper attention to these. It is very easy to reach the last fence and breathe a sigh of relief about completing the jumps but fail to take in the fact that the finishing flags are off-set or further away than you thought. Make sure you look to see exactly where they are from the last fence as, by the time you reach here, you may well be a bit tired so it is vital that you know where to look and aim for the finish.

Carefully assess the area for pulling up in as well, as this is sometimes quite small and you must be able to keep your horse under control on finishing in order to pull him up. Sometimes there is masses of room, so you will need to be able to stop here, rather than sailing off out of control into the distance.

Numbers

Having walked your course, thought it through and seen where everything is for the event, you are all set for action.

Below: **These riders have collected their numbers and are ready to start. Do not forget to hand your number back!**

First, make sure you have your number. At hunter trials these are usually collected from the secretary's tent but occasionally they are located in the horsebox park. Sometimes there is a returnable deposit on these to ensure they are not mislaid for ever! They are normally of the bib type, which come in a variety of sizes, colours and shapes. Some are handed out at the start and then collected on finishing. If you are in a pairs or going as pair but judged as an individual, which occasionally happens, a coloured sash is often worn to aid identification by the judges. If collecting the number at the start, allow time to sort yourself out as, in most cases, it is safer to get off to put it on rather than have flapping tapes etc. put on over your head, which might prove dangerous.

Warming up

All horses need a gentle warm up before doing anything, so work your horse in walk, trot and canter for ten minutes before having a jump. Remember the purpose of what you are doing. The horse needs to be warmed up and loose, ready for the big test. He does not need to be galloped around and jumped end- lessly so that he is half-exhausted before he starts. Two to three jumps should be ample if you have worked him steadi- ly beforehand. A short sharp canter, to make him really stride out and open his lungs, should be done not less than ten min- utes before you actually start. Thereafter, keep him moving in walk until you are due to go.

Don't let your horse stand around before starting. When you know how many competitors there are before you, get your horse warmed up. Trot and canter for five to ten minutes, do a couple of jumps and then keep him walking until you set off.

147

Should there be a delay for any reason, remember to have another brisk trot or canter around before you set off, to ensure that your horse has not fallen asleep. Try to keep yourself as calm as possible by running through your course or watching others if you can see the course from where you are. If you hear of any problems do not let them worry you; just make your aim to come in straight at all fences and ride with determination and to go out and show people how it should be done.

Occasionally there is a starting box to set off from and this should not be entered too early. Keep your horse circling in front of it to keep you both calm and then only go in when the starter is ready to send you on your way. He or she will normally do a count down from five. More usually, you will start between flags but, again, keep walking quietly in a circle until the signal comes to set off on the course.

On the course

Now is the time to prove that all your hard work has been worth it. Keep your head and ride as you had planned on your course walk. If it is sticky going or you are not sure how fit your horse is, take him steadily so as not to wear him out early on the course. If he is feeling full of running half-way round, you can push on a little. It is, however, much better to finish fresh and ready to go again than to have exhausted your horse early on. If you are not that experienced, just remember to keep up a steady rhythm and let the horse dictate the stride. As you do more competing, you will soon start to get a feel for what you and your horse are capable of and will aim higher next time.

Try to learn a bit from each ride: how your horse responds to the different fences, whether you met your fences smoothly and jumped them easily. Was it easy to keep him balanced and under control or do you need to adjust your control system before next time. Pay particular attention to your horse's fitness as well as your own. Neither of you should be unduly tired and you should both be breathing normally shortly afterwards. If may take your horse five to ten minutes to stop puffing but he should have recovered enough to look comfortable and relaxed by that time.

Aftercare of the horse

Once you have pulled up after your round, which should be

done gradually, with a tightish rein, to prevent your horse tripping or stumbling as he slows down, bring him back to a walk and get off. Loosen your girths and run up your stirrups to prevent them catching onto things, such as gate hooks, or knocking your horse's elbows. Lead him around quietly, even while talking to your supporters, so that he is not allowed to stiffen up while hot and sweaty. It is most important for your horse to be given time to wind down after his exertions. He should be led quietly back to the box and have his saddle

Be determined and positive round your course and get straight at every fence. Some, like this one, are in the middle of a field and have no wings, so it is vital to keep your horse straight and going forward.

149

removed. Check him over carefully for any sign of injury, paying particular attention to his legs and heels and any little nicks on his pasterns or fetlocks, which are prone to minor injuries. Make sure he looks sound as you lead him back to the box. If there is anything more than minor bumps or cuts, ask for the vet.

If it is a mild day, he could be sponged down lightly over his neck and saddle patch. Avoid his loins, behind the saddle, as this is a very sensitive area and his long back muscles could go into painful spasm if you use cold water while he is still hot. Be as quick as you can if you want to wash him down, scraper him off and then put a sweat rug or light towelling sheet on, secured with a surcingle, to lead him around in until he has quite recovered.

Offer your horse short drinks once he has stopped puffing hard. A quarter of a bucket every five to ten minutes until he

Walking out in-hand after a hard day is a pleasant way of giving your horse a day off to recover from his efforts.

is satisfied will be much appreciated. If you have not already done so, remove any boots or bandages, studs, etc., and rub his legs lightly with a towel to dry them and stimulate circulation in the area. Once he seems settled and calm, he can have a haynet and be left to rest. However, do add an extra rug if it is cold, as this is the time when he will quickly start to feel it following his exertions. Now is the time to sort yourself out and go and celebrate (or commiserate on!) your round. Do not forget to return your number cloth if you have not already done so.

Travel your horse home as soon as is practical and lead him around to stretch his legs before putting him back in the stable. If he is to go straight out in the field, check his legs again to make sure you have not missed anything and let him loose with a nice, small but appetizing feed. If it is cold and wet, put on a New Zealand rug for the night if you get back late as it is rather unkind to have given him so much attention at the competition and then abandon him into the wet and cold just when he needs a bit of comfort. He will be fine with the rug to keep his back warm. The stabled horse should be given a quick brush over to make him comfortable and have his night rugs put on. Some people prefer to put bandages on overnight for extra warmth and support, others check the legs and rub them or brush them to remove any mud or sweat. He may be thirsty on returning, so let him drink his fill but not too much at one time. Feed him and then check him again later.

Clothes for hunter trials

There is an accepted code of dress for hunter trials, which is basically 'ratcatcher' or tweed coats, hunting boots and skull caps. While this remains popular, the advent of back protectors has resulted in many people being unable to wear their coats on top of these, so cross country dress is becoming more and more usual and either is now acceptable.

Several points are worth considering when it comes to dress, both from the point of view of safety as well as appearance. Skull caps, correctly fastened, are now more or less compulsory everywhere and, speaking from personal experience, I cannot recommend them too highly. You can buy a variety of types but choose one that conforms to recognized safety standards. The chin straps can be made of leather or of a toughened ribbon with a chin guard. It is a matter of personal preference. Some people find the chin guards rather uncomfortable and they can cause bruising. It seems to depend very

A tweed hacking jacket with a blue or black skull cap is always correct for hunter trials. Cross country clothes are, however, now quite acceptable although very bright colours are inappropriate. Back protectors should also be worn.

much on the make and shape of your chin! You can find chin strap attachments in most saddler, should you need a change. If you are wearing a tweed coat you should only wear a dark blue or black silk. If in cross country clothes the choice is yours and many people like to adopt their own 'colours' to wear.

A back protector is highly recommended and for some events is compulsory. The waistcoat variety is probably the most satisfactory. It should be light and comfortable and easy to put on and take off. Most people wear these under their sweaters or coats but they can just as easily be worn on top of the former. Nowadays, it is possible to get some designs in your own colours. It seems really short-sighted not to wear a back protector whenever schooling or competing over cross country fences and they certainly prevent endless bumps or bruises although they will not necessarily help in every situation.

A stock (hunting tie) should be worn when riding cross country as it gives both support and protection to the vulnerable neck area. It is not until you have actually felt what it is like to be scratched and bruised round your neck, especially when galloping through woods where low branches and twigs are liable to be encountered, that you realize the significance of the stock. I never ride cross country without one and have a variety of colours and designs. A subtle-coloured one is correct with a tweed coat but white or any other colour is fine with cross country colours. Once tied, the stock should be secured with a pin placed at any angle or horizontally but never straight up and down,which could bruise your chin or chest if knocked up or downwards.

Gloves should be of a non-slip variety. The string type or 'pimple' gloves are cheap and excellent for their non-slip qualities. Wool is also good. Non-slip gloves are particularly important if you have plain leather reins but if you use non-slip reins, the type of glove is less important. Leather on leather, however, can be suicidal on a strong, sweaty horse.

Safety on the horse

As far as the horse is concerned, it is vital that you have the right amount of control, so an effective bridle, strong and with all stitching in good condition, is priority number one. The bit and noseband should be of the right size for your horse.

A martingale, breastplate with martingale attachment or

153

Method A

 1

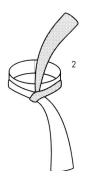 2

 3

 4

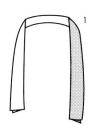 5

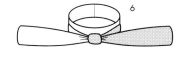 6

 7

Method B

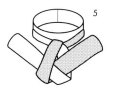 1

2

3

4

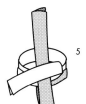 5

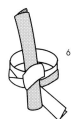 6

 7

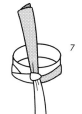 8

 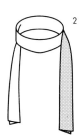 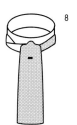

Left: **Tying a stock correctly takes some practice. Both these methods work quite well. Pull the knot fairly tight before arranging neatly and then put the stock pin in horizontally.**

breastplate should be correctly adjusted to perform its function – the former for control; the latter to ensure that the saddle cannot slip back. Breastplates or breastgirths should always be worn for cross country in my opinion. I have seen too many accidents when these have either not been used at all or have been too loosely adjusted to be effective. They should be tight enough to ensure the saddle cannot slip back more than a couple of inches but not so tight that they hinder the shoulder movement.

The surcingle, or overgirth, helps to hold the saddle in place, acts as a safety girth in case your girths snap and holds the saddle flaps down. They are a useful addition if your horse is not too fidgety but, to be really effective, they need to be tightened once you are on top. Sometimes this becomes more of a problem than its value warrants if you cannot get a helper to do it up for you. The buckle should be secured centrally between the horse's legs, not to one side where it could bruise your horse's elbow. It must also never be fastened anywhere near your own leg where it could really interfere with your riding and leave a very painful bruise.

Boots or bandages on your horse's legs are a matter of preference. Horses that are good, straight movers and not prone to knocks or cuts are often best left as they are, especially if they are obedient and easy to manage. Boots are designed to protect the horse from cuts and bruising, so they should be strong and lightweight. The joints, backs of the tendons and fronts of the cannons are the most vulnerable spots, so choose a type that will protect these parts most effectively.

Bandages, if used, are designed for the same basic purpose but also give a little support to the legs, although some people question whether this works in reality. It is unlikely that it does if leg 'shells' are used underneath. These are protective moulds made of a shock-absorbing, porous material, which are fitted round the legs and then bandaged in position. The bandage, which is best if elasticated, should be firmly and evenly applied from just below the knee to just over the actual joint but not below it. It must be carefully secured with insulation tape over the tapes or Velcro as either can come undone if the going is deep or they are caught by the opposite leg. Bandaging over gamgee or other padding is really for the expert as a lot of harm can be done through uneven bandaging, causing damage to tissue and tendons from uneven pressure.

Overreach boots, sometimes called bell boots, are a good precaution, especially if your horse is prone to overreaches

This smartly turned out rider is using sensible tack on her horse, including a breastplate, boots and overreach boots.

from his hind feet catching the heels of his front feet. These are particularly likely in deep ground. The rubber overreach boots come in different sizes and are pulled on inside out and then turned back. Some varieties fasten round the pastern and should be well fitting. Certain types have fixings down the side of the boot, which are not recommended in case the horse catches a foot on these. If using the pull-on variety, they should be taken off by resting the foot on your knee (put a pad underneath), then, with both hands, grasp the top and ease it off over the foot. It can be a struggle but, with practice, you can soon learn the knack.

Studs are a great help on slippery ground, especially when it is very hard as well. In good going they are usually unnecessary, while if it is very deep, their effect is questionable.

For hard going, small, sharp studs are used and there are a variety to choose from. For slippery going, large studs are best. Generally, people use big studs behind and smaller in front if they use front studs at all.

Always clean out the stud holes the day before you go to your event so that they are quick and easy to put in on the day. Use a pointed nail to wiggle around in the stud hole to clear out any surface dirt. If you filled the hole with oiled cotton wool after your last event, this should be relatively easy to get out. Blow hard into the hole to clear it out and then use your 'tap' to ensure the thread is clear. Be careful not to cross-thread this or it will be really difficult to get the studs in. These should be kept well oiled and free from rust so that they go in easily. Use your spanner to tighten them in position.

To take them out, simply unscrew them with the spanner. Fill the holes with oiled cotton wool which should be ready for use in your stud box. Do not forget that your farrier will only put stud holes in if you ask him specifically. As he will charge more for these, remember to tell him when you no longer require them.

Always check all your tack regularly to ensure that everything is in good condition and strong. It is worth taking time over this and to do it several weeks before you want to compete. Look at all the stitching and buckles. Check that the leather is supple and in good condition. It should be soft but not so soft that it will be too flexible.

Do not forget to look at your girth straps high up where they are stitched. Also look at your stirrup leathers and any stitching on girths or boots. Sort out everything that needs attention. Velcro may need replacing and/or the surface cleaned of fluff. Scratch this out with a large darning needle if necessary.

Numnahs can become threadbare quite quickly and should be replaced before they give your horse a sore back. It is always worth having a special one for competing so that you can keep this well brushed or washed. Make sure the straps are secured and restitch them if they start to come loose. Make it a routine after every outing to check everything over and clean it well and put any specific competition gear away ready for your next event.

The next day

The day after your event, carefully check your horse over and notice if he has lost much weight. This is bound to happen, especially with young or excitable horses, but should be barely noticeable with an older, more experienced horse. After a couple of days, he should be back to normal. Check the legs and give them a good feel over for any scabs or signs of injury which may have manifested themselves overnight. Pick out the feet carefully and check the shoes.

Take your horse out for a good walk to stretch his legs, either led or ridden, or turn him out. Give him a thorough grooming to remove any sweat marks, paying particular attention to the elbow area and up inside the hind legs as well as the head area. A gentle rub with your hand will be as effective as anything here and is more comfortable for the horse if he is rather sensitive.

If there are any minor injuries or small cuts, clean them well and spray them with an antibacterial spray. Feel that both legs are even in temperature and size. Pain and heat will indicate a problem, so assess the situation carefully and, if necessary, call your vet. It may be only a bruise but, if around the tendon area, it could possibly be a strain which is potentially quite serious.

If he looks and feels well, your horse will be able to carry on as normal and his feeding routine can more or less remain unchanged but give him slightly smaller feeds for the day or two after an event when he will be having a slightly easier time. One day off, followed by two or three days of steady work before any more jumping, will help his system, muscles and joints to recover from his exertions and any stiffness. It will, in fact, probably be you who is the stiff one!

CHAPTER 5

PRACTICAL HEALTH CARE

The ability to be able to assess a situation and act promptly whenever there is a problem, injury or sign of illness is essential for the caring horse owner. If you can spot things at the outset, you will save yourself much time and money. Make yourself observant at all times and learn to watch how your horse reacts and responds to injury and illness. Usually you can tell quite quickly if something is not quite right just by looking at your horse's face. Ask yourself if his eyes look bright and if he presents a picture of health, with a good loose feel to his coat, standing up and moving evenly on all four legs. Has he staled normally and do his droppings appear as usual in colour, consistency, amount and smell? Any change in these may indicate that something is not quite right. Very often the horse that is feeling a bit off or in pain has a slightly puckered look above his nostrils.

Every horse owner should have a thermometer in the stable and know how to use it. The horse's normal temperature is around 37.5° − 38.5°C (100° − 100.5°F). When you take him temperature, the horse should be at rest, as the temperature will be raised after exercise. After ensuring that the mercury level has been shaken down well, grease the bulb of the thermometer and insert this end gently into the rectum with a slight 'turning' action. Hold it in place for one to two minutes then gently withdraw it and read it.

The horse's pulse is also a useful indicator and this is usually around 35 − 40 beats a minute when the animal is resting. This is normally felt by feeling the artery that passes under the inside of the jawbone or the one in the middle of the inside of the forearm, more or less level with the elbow.

The respiration rate is best recorded by either watching the nostrils or the rise and fall of the flanks as the horse breathes in and out. At rest this should be around eight to sixteen complete breaths a minute.

If any of the above appear abnormal after the horse has competed and remain so, or for any temperature that goes above 102°C at any time, the vet should be called. He or she should also be called if your horse shows any of the following symptoms:

Colic

This is a term used for pain in the belly, which presents with restlessness, raised pulse as the pain builds up, looking and kicking at the stomach and rolling. Keep the horse on his feet as rolling could cause more problems. Either quietly walk him around outside or remain with him, moving him a little as necessary to keep him from rolling. Once you have called the vet, remain with your horse, to watch and observe him. The vet will want to know if he has staled normally, when his last dropping was and whether this was normal, whether he has been gorging on straw and whether his diet has varied recently (i.e. new hay, feed, grass, etc.). Have you heard any bowel sounds (tummy rumblings)?

Coughing or flu symptoms

If your horse is coughing persistently, has a badly running nose and/or a temperature, he may have a virus, flu or a bad cough which requires treatment. To work a horse in such a state can do a lot of harm to his lungs and heart as well as aggravate the symptoms. Rest the horse, take his temperature and, if raised, or if the coughing persists, call the vet. Isolate the horse if possible and keep him warm. Do not allow his water bucket, feed bowl, etc. or bridle to be used by any other horses.

Cuts

Minor cuts can be carefully washed off, gently hosed, then dusted with wound powder or sprayed with antiseptic spray to dry them off. More serious cuts, and particularly puncture wounds, may require stitching and an antitetanus injection as well as antibiotics and pain relievers. Always call your vet in such cases. For these injuries, it is best to cold hose gently and leave the wound or, if bleeding is profuse, cover it with a clean dressing and bandage it firmly. Never spray or cover wounds with powders etc. if they are to be seen by the vet as

Cold hosing is excellent for cuts and to clean wounds and reduce inflammation.

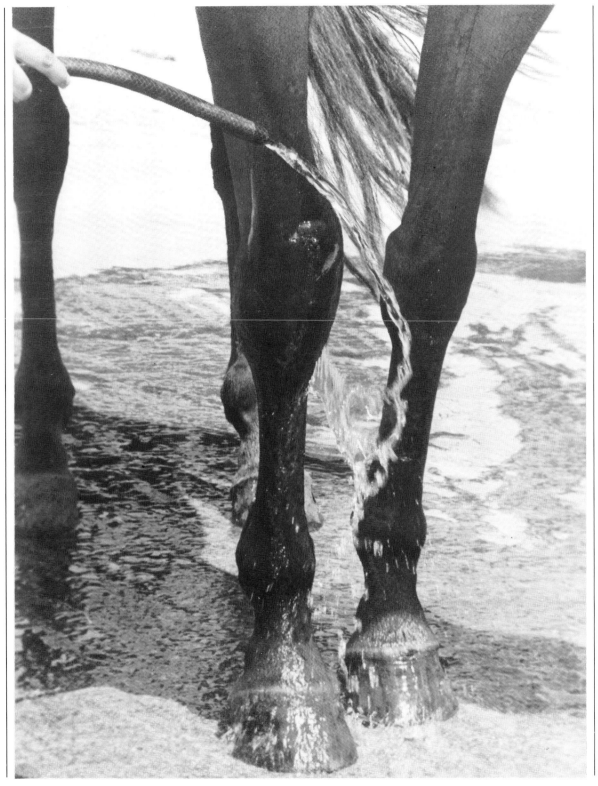

it will be much more difficult for him to assess what needs to be done.

Severe bleeding

Severe bleeding, or that involving a cut artery, requires immediate action. Arterial bleeding spurts out blood as the heart pumps. (A vein bleeds as a continuous flow.) This must be controlled by applying firm pressure over the wound between the wound and the heart. To do this, make a pad from whatever is handy if you do not have a first aid pack with you. A tightly folded handkerchief or even a flat stone pressed against the artery and secured or held firmly to constrict the flow could help to save life. Tourniquets should be loosened every ten to fifteen minutes, then retightened if bleeding recommences, until skilled help arrives. Call the vet immediately.

Bruises

Bruises are best cold hosed gently over the area two or three times daily. Witch hazel applied as a compress, or cold kaolin, is soothing after hosing. After approximately 48 hours the affect of cold treatments is less effective and then some hot kaolin poulticing, for a couple of days, will help to dispel the swelling. The vet will rarely be needed for normal bruises but if there is a large amount of bruising, which forms a haematoma (severe bleeding into tissue), apply ice packs to the area to help to stop the bleeding and call your vet as antibiotics may be required to prevent secondary infection.

Strained tendons

This is a serious injury and will always require the vet to assess the degree of damage. They present as hot and painful around the backs of the tendons, depending on where the strain has occurred. Lameness may or may not be present. The first thing to do is to try to prevent the area getting worse. Ice packs – frozen peas are excellent if nothing else is available – applied to the area and keeping the horse quiet until the vet arrives are the best courses of action. Cold hosing or cold water bandages are also helpful if ice is not available.

Azoturia

This is a very painful condition affecting the muscles of the horse, which seize up into a type of cramp. Those affected are the back and quarter muscles in particular. This condition often occurs after the horse has had a day off but his feed has not been cut down but this is not necessarily the only reason. The horse may start off perfectly all right and then start to stagger or drag his hind legs and generally become reluctant to move. He may sweat profusely with the pain. Get off immediately and keep him as still as possible. In most cases he will not want to move anyway but movement can seriously increase the damage already being done to his muscles as blood vessels become damaged by the spasm.

Get help immediately and call the vet, leaving the horse where he is if necessary unless you can get transport back. Keep him warm. Should he stale, this is likely to be very dark with the appearance of coffee grounds. The vet will take a blood test to determine the amount of muscle damage present, which will then determine the course of action to take as the horse recovers. Afterwards, you should look seriously at your work load in relation to your feeding programme and assess whether you are giving your horse too much protein and whether you should cut down by giving only a bran mash before a day off. For some horses just a little too much food can tip the balance in the wrong direction and never forget that it is always safer to give too little rather than too much when it comes to food concentrates. It cannot be overstressed that a lot more harm is done through overfeeding than underfeeding.

Foot injuries

These are common and often result in sudden and acute pain. If a stone is caught in the foot, usually wedged between the frog and the shoe, this can normally be dealt with immediately with little damage done. Get off the horse at once and pick out the foot. You may have to find a strong stick or another sharp stone to use as a hoof pick. Once the stone is removed, the horse should go sound again unless there has been severe bruising as well.

Abscesses

These can develop in the foot and are usually caused by bruising at some earlier stage. They can be excruciatingly painful when the pressure builds up to the point where there is no further room for swelling as the hoof cannot expand like other parts of the body.

The foot will be hot and the horse will be quite lame and reluctant to put his weight on it. The inflammation has to be relieved by allowing the abscess to drain, so your farrier or the vet should be called to decide how this should be done. Hot poulticing, to draw out the pus, will be necessary, as will tubbing in a bowl of hot water containing salt to help with the drawing-out affect.

Punctured sole

Occasionally, a horse will pull or half-pull his shoe off and then tread on the nail, causing a puncture wound. This will also usually result in an abscess unless an antibiotic is given immediately to prevent one forming. Generally, antibiotics are not a great success with foot injuries as they appear to disguise the injury rather than really clearing it up but every case is different and your vet will decide what is best.

Overreaches

Overreaches to the heel area are extremely common and are normally caused by the hind foot catching the heels of the front one, resulting in severe bruising to the area and often some nasty cuts to the bulbs of the heels. These should be thoroughly cleaned out and, if necessary, poulticed if the cut is very dirty but not for too long as this will only tend to soften the heel. Antibacterial spray or powder will help to dry up the area. Keep your horse out of dirt and mud until this has healed over and keep it clean. Cream may be useful if the area is very dry.

Cracked heels

This is another, equally maddening, condition that arises for a number of reasons. It may be caused by soreness, caused by standing in muddy conditions for long periods of time, or by dryness of the skin, causing cracking in this vulnerable area. An infection or virus can affect the area and certain soils appear to cause irritation.

Wash the area thoroughly and use a mild soap in warm water. Rub the scabs off gradually as they become softened by the soap and water. If the scabs are not loosened in one or two sessions, you will need to continue the treatment daily until every scab is gone. Carefully dry the area and apply an antibacterial cream. Keep the heels as dry and as clean as possible until the condition clears. White legs tend to be far more prone to this.

Sores

These can be some of the most difficult conditions to treat as they are usually caused by friction to an area that is sensitive. The most common sites are the corners of the mouth, which can be caused by an ill-fitting bit, rough hands or friction. Bathe the area and apply a little cream. Remove the cause. A few days without a bridle is likely to be necessary.

Sore backs are caused by many different things, such as a badly fitting saddle or one that has a broken tree or requires restuffing. The horse may be in soft condition and has not hardened up sufficiently to cope with the weight and movement of the rider, or with one who moves a lot or sits unevenly in the saddle. Find the cause and try to sort that out first. Treat the area with surgical spirit unless the skin is broken, when a wound spray may be more appropriate. Rest the back and start riding with appropriate padding, such as an extra thick numnah or gel pad, once this has settled.

Some rubs and sores develop from 'boot rubs', caused by friction in most cases. Carefully clean the area and apply wound powder, spray or cream as appropriate. Question the necessity to use boots if this is a regular problem. Put them on only for schooling or when the horse is at its most vulnerable. If your horse is a good mover, he will be unlikely to knock himself too often but, if not, then some protection will be necessary. Ask your farrier if he can help with special shoeing if this is a big problem. You may then be able to leave boots off for some of the time, giving the legs a bit of a rest.

First aid cupboard

A well-stocked first aid cupboard is vital in every stable and never more so than in one where horses are competing. Always have the vet's number written up clearly as well as a notebook and pen, so that you can jot it down and hand it someone who could help in an emergency. This goes for the doctor, as well, as it is not only the horse that gets injured should an accident occur.

Keep everything neat and tidy and restock any items immediately they run out. You should have at least the minimum amount detailed below and anything else that you have found to be useful in the past.

1 Dressings – a variety of different sizes and, if possible, some non-stick ones. Animalintex is universally used for wounds.

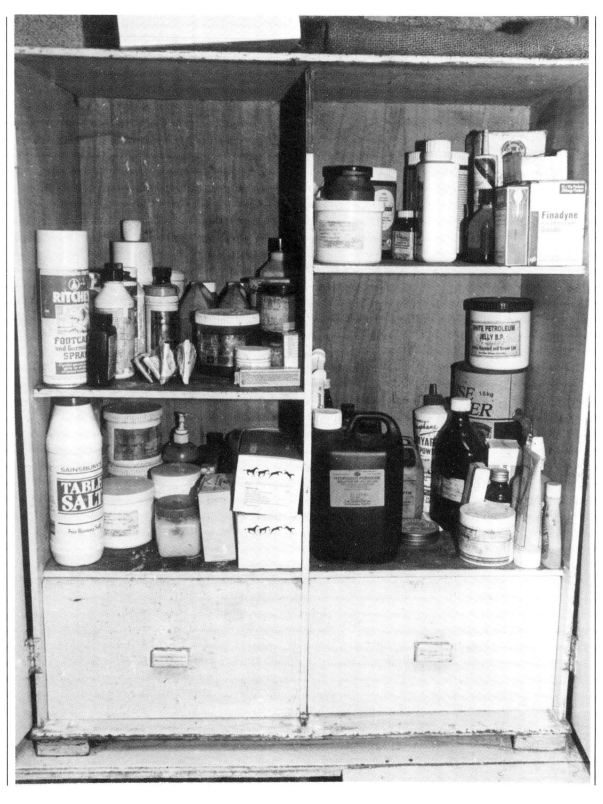

A well stocked first aid cupboard is a must for every stable. Stocks should be replenished as soon as they run out.

2 Bandages – a couple of crêpe or stretchy bandages should be included to hold any dressings in place. Also gamgee for padding.
3 Scissors – a sharp pair that will cut dressings and a curved, blunt-ended pair to cut hair from around a wound.
4 Surgical tape or plaster helps to hold dressings in place if they are prone to slipping down.
5 Cotton wool and a bowl or bucket to clean out wounds.
6 Hydrogen peroxide is excellent for cleaning wounds as it removes dried blood or serous fluid as it bubbles up round the wound. It must be diluted to the instructions on the bottle. Salt is also excellent to clean out wounds or for use as a mild antiseptic solution.
7 Wound sprays, powders or creams. These should be used as recommended by your vet for healing and have an antibacterial action.
8 A thermometer is essential and should be placed some-where safe.
9 Kaolin for poulticing is also a horseman's must. You will need pieces of cut-up brown paper or something similar (feed sacks are ideal) on which to spread this, and also some plastic covering.
10 Stockholm tar is commonly used for foot problems and for sealing punctures to the foot once an abscess has drained. Use rubber gloves.
11 Rubber gloves, or plastic ones if preferred, for use when dealing with injuries.
12 Clean towels for use on the horse to dry off wounds. Also for the vet when he washes his hands.

Poulticing

As poulticing is such a common necessity when dealing with horses, it is worth being quite clear about what is involved and the main points to consider when using one. Poultices are used to draw out infection, reduce inflammation and bruising and generally clean wounds. They can be applied hot or cold, dry or wet depending on the type used.

Kaolin poultices are used mostly for inflammation, bruising and to ease jarring to the legs. They can be applied cold or hot. The easiest method consists of spreading the kaolin on to some brown paper cut to the size of the area to be covered – generally on the leg. It can be stiff to spread. If a cold poultice is required, this can be applied with a sheet of plastic on

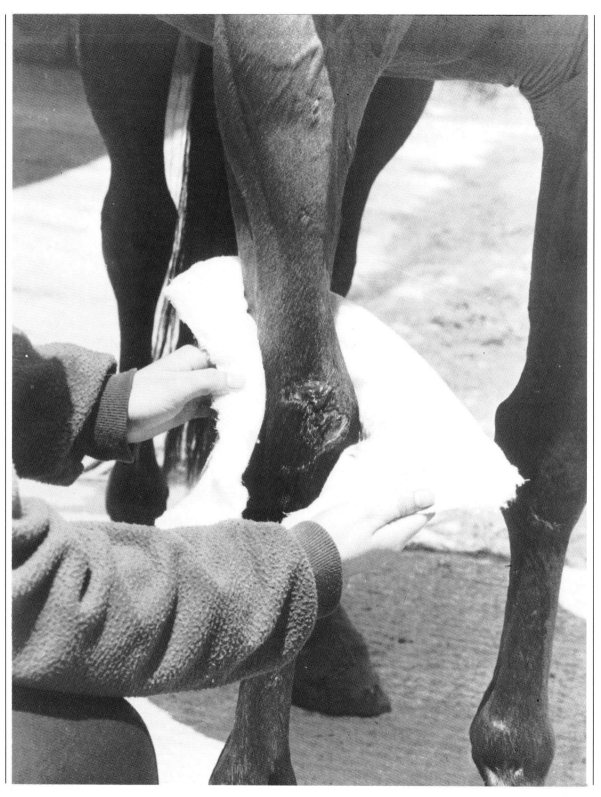

Applying poultices to injuries requires practice but poultices are essential to help keep wounds clean.

the outside and bandaged in place. If hot kaolin is required, heat it in the oven or under a grill for one to two minutes. It should be applied when comfortably hot (not tepid). Never put it on the horse without testing on yourself to make sure that it will not be too hot when in place. If you are unable to use this method and you have a tin of kaolin, you can heat the tin up in a pan of boiling water and then spread and use it. Always cover it with plastic to prevent leakage round the edges and to help to keep the heat in. Cling film is useful for this or else plastic bags can be cut up and wrapped round.

Animalintex is a complete poultice on its own and the directions on the bag indicate how it should be used. Cut it to the size required, pour on boiling water (or cold), squeeze out any surplus water, test it for heat, apply it to the area and bandage it in place.

Foot poultices can be used with either of the above, as well as making up a bran poultice. Mix bran in the corner of a sack etc. with a tablespoon of Epsom salts, and pour boiling water over this. Drain off any excess water, test that it is not too hot and pack it into the foot around the affected area. Cover it with plastic and padding and bandage it in place. An Equiboot may be fitted over the top to keep the poultice in place if it will fit.

Prevention

Accidents and injuries can happen at any time but it can never be overstressed that prevention is better than cure. With all the time and effort that goes into competing, there is nothing more disappointing than missing out due to an avoidable injury. The golden rule is never to take risks. Never get into the habit of not bothering about something because it will 'probably be all right just this once'. Keep your horse regularly shod as overlong feet or loose shoes can cause injury so easily. Keep fencing, stabling and equipment in a good state of repair.

Think before you act – it is so easy to rush off on an impulse to jump a fence that you know is too big and undermine all those hours of confidence-building when things go wrong. Learn to look ahead and foresee problems before they arise. However, do not become over anxious; if you are sensible and you have done your best, this will usually be good enough.

Never think you know it all – no one does! There is always so much to learn when riding, training and competing with horses, so always be prepared to accept help and criticism. At least try out suggestions and see if anything works better for you. Most people only offer help if they genuinely feel you need it or if they foresee an accident looming – either way, it is likely to be to your advantage.

Look ahead to the future. If you have done well in hunter trials at all levels, you may want to think of being more ambitious over your fences. The sport of horse trials requires a dedicated all-rounder who is brave enough to tackle more complicated and bigger fences, and who is prepared to take on the different schooling necessary for dressage and show jumping.

CHAPTER 6

COPING WITH COMMON PROBLEMS

Inevitably, somewhere along the way, problems will arise for a variety of reasons. It is essential that you can identify the cause if you are to overcome these. The more you come up against and cope with, the more you will learn. There is no better way of learning than through your own mistakes. Identify the cause, then find the remedy. The following may help with some of the more common problems.

Horses not going forward

This is probably the most common fault to be found anywhere. If your horse is not pulling a little and he is not up in front of your leg, then he is not going forward. The cause may be lack of training or lack of impulsion and push from you, the jockey. Are you being just a passenger? Some horses require more motivation from the rider before they show enthusiasm, so use your legs more effectively. He may be bored and fed up because you have overdone the jumping or schooling and needs some variation or a break.

Your horse may not be fit enough and is tired or not having enough food for what you are expecting of him. Work him little and often rather than for too long at a time. You may be expecting too much but, even if young, the first, most important lesson for every animal to learn is that of going forward. Are you overbitting him so that he is frightened of doing so? Choose a milder bit and make sure you have sympathetic hands.

Really work on getting your horse going forward into a consistent rhythm – he must respond to your leg aids and go forwards and come back to you when you ask him.

A rider losing balance

This will affect the horse's way of going as the horse will not be receiving the consistent aids required to keep him working evenly because the rider keeps adopting different positions to counter their lack of balance. One of the causes may be riding with overlong stirrups. Shorten these a little, push your weight down more into the heel and find your balance by bringing your body forwards a little before sitting more upright. Some people tend to lean back, which makes it very difficult to remain balanced if your lower leg position is not secure. The same can be said if you get too far forwards.

An unbalanced horse

This is usually the result of lack of direction from the rider. The horse needs to be rebalanced with a series of half-halts and stronger leg aids to engage the quarters. Make him more obedient through more positive and effective use of your legs, seat and hands.

Straightness

This is another aspect that affects everything you do. If the horse is not straight in his way of going, he must be straightened through suppling exercises and correct balancing. The leg and hand must be used together to influence the horse to go straight. This may need quite a lot of work. Remember that it is the legs that control the quarters, and, together with the hands, the balance and speed. A little more left leg will need to be exerted if the horse brings his quarters in to the left and vice versa. For the horse to meet his fences correctly, it is vital that he learns to go straight at all times.

Jumping problems

These usually stem from any of the aforementioned problems on the flat so it is essential that the basic principles are looked at every time a problem occurs. Is the horse going forward, is he straight, does he have impulsion and balance? Is the rider being consistent in their riding? Keep asking yourself these basic questions every time you encounter problems.

If the horse is not going forward, he will not have the impulsion to go easily over a fence. The result may be that he will refuse, have to make an effort to jump the fence, get straddled over the fence, etc. This will all lead to lack of confidence for both horse and rider. Check all reasons, assess what the real problem is and act accordingly, taking a positive approach.

If the horse is not straight, he is liable to jump the fence on the angle or run out at some stage. Either is incorrect and will increase the difficulty. The jump becomes wider if jumped on the angle and, once the horse has run out, he will soon learn bad habits. It is a nightmare once an intelligent horse has learnt to take advantage. Be quick to correct him, shorten your reins, use your legs and make sure you are the boss whenever he tries to run out.

Balance and impulsion will fall into place as long as you have forward movement combined with a consistent rhythm. Use your legs and push your horse up into the hand. Keep him balanced and always working forward. Refer to Chapter 2 if you are not achieving success and try to see what it is that is missing.

Consistent riding is most important as the horse comes to rely on his rider after a time and needs to build up this trust. This will be very difficult to achieve with a rider who is checking one moment and throwing all to the wind the next. Keep an even, soft contact with your hand and a firm, consistent leg.

Once you have a firm lower leg, spurs can be helpful for the more sluggish type of horse. A stick should be carried at all times when training and competing so that you have the necessary aids should problems arise.

The information gained from this book should enable you to learn a lot about riding across country and competing in hunter trials as well as about the relevant care associated with the sport. There is nothing more exciting than riding over daunting fences and feeling that wonderful power of the horse as he soars into the air, making it all seem so easy. This, however, does not come about without a lot of hard work and dedication and I really hope this book has been a helpful and practical guide on what to do and how to go out there and enjoy doing it with confidence.

INDEX

Page numbers in *italics* refer to captions